Keep ...   U !

all Best Wishes,
Charlotte

Ripples of Air

Poems of Healing

ripples of air

poems of healing

Charlotte Digregorio

Artful Communicators Press
711 Oak St., Ste. 310
Winnetka, IL 60093

Copyright © 2020 by Charlotte Digregorio.

All rights reserved. No part of this book may be reproduced or transmitted in any form or by any means, electronic or mechanical, including photocopying, recording or by any information storage and retrieval systems, without written permission from the publisher, except for the inclusion of brief quotations in a review.

Published by:
Artful Communicators Press
711 Oak St., Ste. 310
Winnetka, IL 60093, U.S.A.

Library of Congress Control Number: 2019952118

ISBN: 978-0-9912139-1-7

Printed and Bound in the United States of America

Dedication

~

I dedicate this book to people
who appreciate the healing nature of poetry
and to those who will discover
its form of healing in reading it.

Charlotte Digregorio

About
Ripples of Air:
Poems of Healing

~

Charlotte Digregorio has the all-too-uncommon ability to put the reader in the poet's place. One does not read, so much as experience her poems. Closing my eyes, many of these poems could have been memories from my own past. These very personal poems become personal to the reader. The poet uses words as her brush, and all senses are stimulated.

— Ignatius Fay, Poet & Co-Author, *Breccia*

An affecting collection. Charlotte Digregorio finds lyricism in solitude, finds reason to celebrate and transform into art the trifles in our gritty lives. These are poems of great skill, poems with a generous heart by a writer who cherishes the luminous particulars of every moment.
— Marsh Muirhead, Poet & Author, *last night of the carnival*

Nuanced by childhood memories of oceans and jagged monoliths, of black bear and elk, Charlotte Digregorio shares through reflection and meditation, poems with a spaciousness that speak of acceptance and gratitude for what is. She is like the sculptor in one of her poems, "creating equilibrium and harmony." Digregorio reaches out and invites the reader to join her in solitude, share thoughts and observations. There's an exuberance of life here that cannot help but touch you.

— Mary Jo Balistreri, Poet & Author, *Still*

Award-winning poet Charlotte Digregorio offers readers an array of poems that delve deeply into the external, her Midwest surroundings, and the internal, the nature of her creativity. Digregorio's delectable collection is one to be savored again and again.

— Roberta Beary, Poet & Author, *The Unworn Necklace*

The poems of Charlotte Digregorio possess a clarity of vision one seldom finds in contemporary verse. The images she creates are vibrant and alive. We Baby Boomers identify with her all too well.

— John J. Dunphy, Poet & Author, *Touching Each Tree*

Acknowledgments

~

I sincerely thank Vickie Swisher of Studio 20/20
in Toledo, Illinois for the design and cover of this book.
I am also grateful to Editor-Authors Jennifer Dotson and
Stanford M. Forrester, and Artist-Author Lidia Rozmus
who have shown me many possibilities for creativity,
inspiring me with their dedication
to making the literary arts more visible.

There is poetry in all of us.
Poetry heals.

Contents

~

Appendices

Introduction

~

Poetry Matters: It Is Healing

Readers often skip a book's Introduction to get to the heart of it. I hope you read this.

Poems do matter. They make us aware of life's joys and delights, and they heal life's hurts. When written well, readers can understand them.

Poems that are sad heal us. They allow us to face what ails us: our disappointments, preoccupations, fears, and pain. Poems of joy and humor also heal us. We need both.

We need to heal at various times in our lives, and sometimes even as a daily exercise. We face stress, guilt, illness, trauma, grief, and major losses. We need solitude, at times, to work through our problems. Being outdoors in nature can help us find the quiet we need to heal, or simply looking out the window at nature or viewing art in a museum are healing. Writing poems inspired by these quiet activities is also good for our well-being, if we have the desire.

We find that poems expressing our upset and anger heal us, just by the act of writing them, thus validating our feelings. These expressions using humor can be a healing path.

I sometimes center my healing around my favorite color green, a soothing color, and I write about it. It reminds me of the beauty and colors of nature, and generally, of life's abundance. Trees, leaves, and plants evoke life. We breathe in the pine needles and fresh-mown grass.

Air is life: the first breath of a newborn, the wind, and a breeze with the fragrance of flowers, to name just a few examples. Breathe in air and heal. Feel nature's healing. Hence, the title of this book, "Ripples of Air."

Poems allow us to put our deepest thoughts on paper and connect with others, communicating our common hopes, fears, and dreams, no matter how diverse our lives and cultures. Each poem speaks to us in different ways, as our frame of reference and reactions to it involve our own personal experiences.

Offering a poem to someone is like greeting someone with empathy and compassion. We are fellow travelers through wildernesses that can initially leave us broken or even hopeless. But ultimately, we find glimmers of hope to carry us through our lives with promise, strength, and renewed insight. We learn to find happiness in small triumphs, not only in the large ones, and poetry shows us this.

From short poems like a haiku or cinquain, to longer poetry, the written word validates us. Through poetry, writers share thoughts that can transform us in big ways and small. We discover that a poem provides solace when we realize that poets express our own feelings. Through poetry, we find we are "normal."

No one ever escapes troubles or hardships. When we were children, we often thought our friends had perfect lives. We soon learned they didn't. Perhaps poets can make the earth kinder by tapping into our common sensibilities. Poets show others that we struggle together.

There is poetry in all of us. You, too, can write poetry. As someone who has taught most of my life, I can say that with certainty.

Read and write poems. Poetry is your companion through life. The positive and calm energy you receive from writing poetry will change your life, and spill over into your job, family life, relationships, and sense of self. It's like practicing meditation or yoga.

Wayward Moments

"We do not remember days, we remember moments."

— *Cesare Pavese*

Writers' moments jotted down can be beautiful: morning fog lifting; watching a crashing waterfall from a hilltop; the woodpecker's staccato from an open window; the touch of a ladybug landing on the hand; and blue February sky. It is calming to get lost in the moment and to be grateful for it. As poets, we are told "show, don't tell." We capture moments like a photographer and attempt to describe them in fresh ways.

Some novelists speak of creating significant moments in their work. As a poet, I always carry a pocket notebook, allow moments to happen, and capture them before they escape me.

Significant moments are, at first, often seemingly small or ordinary ones until I stop to closely observe and marvel at how amazing they are.

When sitting alone late at night, I try to remember significant moments of my day. I routinely ask myself what my favorite moment was, and I write about it. A favorite or happy moment is sometimes my lifeline. I don't focus on whether my day was good. I prefer to focus on moments without considering my whole day or entire life, since focusing on moments makes daily living more manageable.

However, if I were to just write about moments without sharing them, I might as well store them in a box. In publishing them, I can engrave common feelings and truths for others, and this is gratifying.

Below, is a tanka I wrote that illustrates this. A tanka, of Japanese origin, is an untitled poem of five lines and a maximum of thirty-one syllables with little or no punctuation or capitalization:

wielding a duster
i hum to a music box
in my memory
wondering how much
of this dust is me

When I record images and share them with readers, I try to describe them precisely. I not only strive to find a fresh angle, but to spur readers' thinking with possible layers of meaning. I attempt to show how I've gotten to the heart of the moment. For example, in discovering my old toy chest in Mother's attic, I found my yo-yo and its string still tangled, just as I'd left it as a child. In teaching my workshops, I note that specific observation makes the experience real for others.

I write the short forms of haiku and senryu, the latter that focuses on human nature, rather than nature as haiku does. These two forms are known for capturing life's moments through which one finds healing and peace. Through haiku and senryu, I use my imagination to explore the moment not only for its beauty and respite, but to seek wisdom. (Haiku and senryu are often one to three lines and untitled, with capitalization and punctuation used sparingly, if at all.)

haiku:

wooded hills . . .
the evening downpour
fogs distant city lights

senryu:

aging . . .
getting the freckles
i wanted in childhood

If I've had a bad day, it's helpful to discover a happy moment in it. But even when I write about a sad moment, it can be healing coming to terms with "the suchness" of life and sharing it with others who may have experienced similar moments. Some people, for example, have experienced the jarring moment of being notified of the sudden death of someone close to them. In writing about it, and reliving that moment, one can find solace, facing one's innermost feelings.

When I write about and share moments, others tell me they recognize ones they've experienced. My moments then belong to them. It's worth the courage it takes to publish sad moments as I'm helping others through similar difficult times.

Here is a haiku I wrote:

winter deepens . . .
my hands warm mother's
limp feet

I also allow readers to participate in my discoveries in nature, such as in a mother duck's vigilance guarding its young in a pond or a spider in sunlight creating its tapestry. A poetry moment can be relatable to others, even if they've never experienced it.

When I "paint" with words, I allow readers to look at life differently. In "painting" life, writers have an affinity with visual artists.

It's hard to live in the moment, as we are often told to do, without fearing the future. Living in the moment is easier if we don't wear a watch or constantly check our electronic devices for the time.

I may view the world differently than others by seeing possibilities in a particular moment that they don't. I ask myself, for example, what's curious or even strange about an ordinary moment such as falling rain. This is a good poetry practice. Recently, I remembered a favorite tune from college in listening to rain. I associated the downpour with the moment of sitting on the carpet of my dorm room listening to James Taylor's tune "Suite for 20G," with the lyric, "Let it rain . . . let it wash your love down all around me." Next, through stream of consciousness, I wondered what had become of a college friend who enjoyed the song. Following moment after moment can be intriguing.

I don't want my moments to escape me. In writing about them, I'm able to focus on my gratitude for the gift of life. I work daily at recording and cultivating the wellspring of ideas that inspire my art.

When I die, all my moments will be set free. I will be like a butterfly on a cherry blossom lifting itself into flight, freeing the moment.

Charlotte Digregorio
Winnetka, Illinois
USA

N.B. In Ripples of Air, the poems of several forms have been published in journals, anthologies, and books and have been reprinted often. Many have won awards. Among the various forms are haiku and senryu sequences (with titles), acrostic, cinquain, Petrarchan sonnet, etheree, and haibun. Many short poems that are untitled and lack capital letters are of the Japanese-style.

Be mindful
of your moments

1 ~ Nostalgia

We all experience nostalgia, yearning for something in our past with fond memories. Perhaps it was a place where we felt carefree, special people we've since lost contact with, or a year where things worked out beautifully for us and our lives were rewarding.

Some of us are nostalgic for where we grew up, having moved from a different part of the country or world. We miss our childhood home, our old school with friends and teachers. Perhaps we miss the scenery of that place— walking through the woods, seeing farm animals, or digging holes in sand along the coast. We miss our childhood pets, our mother's cooking, visits to our grandparents.

For those without strong birthplace connections, perhaps you wish you could return to your younger adult years when life was simpler, you didn't need much money, and you were unencumbered with family obligations. Maybe you had a routine each Friday night and gathered with your friends at a certain place that you miss. Do you miss a former girlfriend or boyfriend and wonder what became of that person? Do you remember your first modest apartment that you called your own place?

Or, perhaps you wish you hadn't moved from a rural area to the metropolis, missing the peace of a slower life where you knew a lot of people.

Regrets are part of life, and writing about them through poetry helps. We often think of past chapters in our lives, the things that have made us who we are—our relatives or former acquaintances who influenced us.

You can write poetry about your nostalgia by perhaps reviewing a journal you've kept and drawing from it. Focus on a person, a place or an event from your past. The beauty of writing a poem, even a short one, is that you can take a "mini-vacation" to your past that was a peaceful or enjoyable time.

Twilight in Winter

After the holidays,
hunched in my leather chair,
the lap robe shawls my back.
Feathers of snow fall quickly
filling the tattered basketball hoop.

Cradling the white cat
nose-deep in his fur,
I remember our old spaniel's
hot breath on my knee.

On the coffee table,
a cranberry candle melts,
dribbles on old china.
I see silence.

The sewing basket,
once holding family together,
half full.

Summer on Lake Michigan

No salt air,
no booming waves,
the folding ocean waves
of my surfer youth.

No jagged monoliths
or coastal mountains of
black bear and elk,
my childhood mysteries.

Just the lake's equilibrium
in morning light and soft air,
small white footprints to trace.

Not even a stone's throw
disturbs the lull.
Ripples float away

with thoughts of my thoughts
reaching sky's end.

First of September

Walking in early morning,
humid air covers the scent
of dahlias and petunias.

Beside the commuter train tracks,
spotted rose leaves and
yellowing maples
surround me.

My mind wanders to frigid winds,
crunching through snow in
ski boots. Passing seasons
and regrets dog me.

For a few moments, I am
a fidgety sixth grader,
carrying a cumbersome binder,
memorizing spelling, believing
grown-ups have all the answers.

Gone now, the stone schoolhouse,
catty classmates, paper stars,
uprooted by a park with
weathered benches, branches
with spoiled pears and apples.

The clickety-clack of wheels distracts me,
morning moon recedes.
In the rear car, standing room only.

Her Chocolate Chip Cookies

Mother wore a crisp white apron
and ardent air. She hummed
hymns, measuring and mixing flour,
eggs, white and brown sugar,
vanilla, chopped walnuts,
and chewy chocolate chips.

She powered her '50s Sunbeam mixer
like a drill, flattening and
whipping a butter cube,
pouring in the other ingredients
for a rich goo. Licking the spatula
gave me a sugar-high.

Now, I slice a log of dough
from the grocery case,
placing the chunks on
mother's aluminum pan.
Baked, the cookies taste
stone-dry, gritty.

The scent of Mother's cookies
wafts through my mind at
the park we used to picnic in.
By the pond, I listen to mallards quack,
and see my reflection as a girl
ripple beside her smooth face.

The Fickle Muse

A co-worker at the factory where
I'd once packed doorknobs, had fine red hair,
a wiry build, but was otherwise as
indistinguishable as a shadow.

He knocked at my flat's door one Sunday
as ink dripped from my finger,
splotching my paper.
He didn't stay long, perhaps sensing
he'd interrupted my writing with talk
about not having a purposeful job.

He had visited a few times before,
once walking with me in brisk air
scented with pine needles.
We listened to withered brown leaves
cartwheeling in the streets.

An occasional walking companion,
we usually didn't have memorable conversations,
yet he came after Mother's death to console me
by reciting unfamiliar scripture.
We climbed wooded hills above the grinding city
until drumming rain cut the outing short.
I walked home alone.

In winter, we were wind-whipped
on shores of the frozen lake.
He wore a ski mask, looking sinister.
On neighborhood streets, when I paused for
sun-streaked oak branches laden with ice,
he became impatient, heading home to shovel snow.

Months later, on the express train,
I spotted him wearing a hobo cap
among motionless faces.
He was reading psalms.

At my stop, he exited. As we walked,
he hummed "Amazing Grace" during silences.
Halfway to my flat, he excused himself.
I was accompanied the rest of the way
by the moon's shadow, shining on snow banks.

In summer at dusk, we strolled
on streets lined with old growth.
He whistled to a tabby.
We climbed the hill with cherry blossoms
and tasted warm wind.

One night, I saw him at a bus stop
wearing overalls and a straw hat.
Stopping for him in my car,
we rode through darkness while
he spoke of wanting to travel
cross-country to find his "soul."
Reaching his trailer park, I wished him well.

The next year, he moved. I heard
he'd left on a bus to "somewhere."

Since his departure forty years ago,
I've been wordful and wordless
on Dad's old Remington,
pounding with four stubby fingers.

His wayward ways still inspire me
during my creative surges.
Many drift onto our path and vanish,
forgotten, but every few years
he knocks at my brain.
I ask where he is and if he's found
purpose, hearing no reply.

Shades of Gray

Mother tells me I should seek peace and happiness.
My first home is a studio in a dilapidated brownstone,
invisible in Portland's fog. The building still has some
charm inside with rustic moldings.

My apartment is dim and dank with a tumbledown
fireplace. A single window looks out onto a fire escape with
autumn rain spurting from rusted gutters. Vintage 1950s
décor, retrieved from mother's moldy attic, includes: a
gray sofa, spotted with coffee; faded green armchairs, his
and her sizes; and a lamp with a long, dust-stained shade.
On my old high school desk, there is a tin of pencils.

There are quirks with apartment living. Every weekend,
the next-door neighbor wails and dances to salsa music.
Often, the elevator is out of order. I climb steep stairs to
the third floor with grocery bags of pasta, potatoes, bread,
apples, and milk.

A part-time teacher and writer, I practice poverty, but
also gratitude for my independence. After a day with
vocal students, I come home and close my eyes for a few
silent moments.

summer on the coast . . .
breezing with
a silver kite

Solace in Early Autumn

On the riverbank, I sun my face
and listen to a singing frog
in breezy calm.

A fawn runs through the woods
to a grassy open patch.
After pausing for moments,
it returns to darkness
fading into old growth.

I board my canoe, row
past deep pines along shore,
refreshing my face in soft winds.

Docking my boat,
I linger in the woods and
eavesdrop on a barred owl,
turning my head from side to side
to locate its call.

I head just beyond to Mother's
old house, vacant since her death.
From the outside, I look in.
Again, she's seated on a high stool,
stirring her tomato sauce
in Grandmother's kettle.

In her garden, I gather figs
in my knapsack until
twilight descends.

I walk to Uncle's house
behind Mother's,
shuffling my shoes through
leafy mounds of scarlet and
yellow as I did in childhood.

At his porch in darkness,
crescent moon disappears
leaving me with stars.

Looking Back

On the prairie
with faraway whistles
of trains,
I feel the pipe waves,
pipe dreams of youth,
see the whale's eye,
and coastal mountains.
Sunrise, my sacred place,
where sea touches sky,
the Eternal.
Afternoon sun
steams my pores,
night breeze
brushes my back
in the ebb
of another life.

Titans

Titans baring concrete,
glass, steel, and stone,
stand in defiance of sky,
rising through swollen clouds
from earth to eternity.

Ever-higher, over-populated,
desolate, soulless.

Dizzying in sunlight
blinding with metal,
they loom over tired shadows
on streets in twilight.

Inside, a captive, I face intruders,
apparitions at windows by day,
silhouettes by night.
Anonymous, I crave
companionship, yet quietude.

No fresh air wild with evergreens,
nor hammocks to doze in,
window boxes with pink dahlias,
violets nor marigolds.

No pears I can pick nor fig trees
to plant. Left with memories
of flitting hummingbirds and
hooting owls camouflaged in poplars.

Holidays diminished, I miss
pumpkins lining my door,
wood fires blowing swirls of smoke,
snow sprinkling holly trees.

Nature's bits and pieces, voices
and echoes buried in gray.

Ode to Borders Books

Dark autumn through radiant summer,
we gathered for poetry open mics,
far from boisterous Chicago cafes
in Highland Park's square.

Borders on Central Street, long defunct,
lost in cumulus clouds.
Some remember the sounds that entertained us.

Performers wove lilting images,
perhaps first written as ink-smudged words
on scraps of paper.

Distinct voices recited sonnets on daily chores
and surreal verse on death by sea serpents
and funerals with apparitions.

Chanters of meditations rippled their tongues
with rhythms of foggy ocean shores,
fertile mountains, and the red-tailed hawk's
circling glide.

Romantics moved us with songs of warm rain,
burgeoning French tulips, and moonlight
through pines.

Spirited satirists, with grand gestures and
sardonic wit, elicited simpers and guffaws
reading ribald limericks.

For poets opening their souls to strangers
and patrons who culled inspiration for
their creative mill, Borders still exists.

We walk by night along the hollow avenue
to the old store. Peering through its windows,
we hear shadows of persistent poets.

Drifting

At the greasy spoon,
flames rise from the grill.
I relish my promotion.

I look out into twilight.
Across the highway,
fog settles over steel tracks
in frozen ground.

I should have left by rail
decades ago, rather than drift
in rain, leaving no footprints.

Living on flat land,
I dream of dazzling ocean,
strewn with rocks and lighthouses,
guarded by emerald peaks.

In my corner, the waitress
interrupts my musings.
She serves joe, tepid and watery,
in a bottomless cup, as the smell
of corn dogs wafts from another table.

Sky darkens,
moonless, starless.
I hear the grinding
on the tracks.

Snapshots

In my waning years, I mindcomb the seasons
of my childhood through young adulthood.

In spring, I chased an orange-spotted butterfly
on the cherry blossom hill, and walked my spaniel in
the forest beside fragrant pines touching summer sky.
In a patch of clovers, autumn-withered, I pretended
I'd found a four-leaf by wrapping my finger and thumb
around two clovers of one and three heads.
At the park, the slide grounded in winter, I imagined
the snowdrifts as mountains. Climbing the slide backwards,
I soaked my boots and pants, and continued
plowing through thigh-deep snow.

In my teens, I scored four baskets from long-range jump shots
in the final game. The coach yelled "You're on fire,"
redemption from my previous zero-point games.
On summer break, under slothful sky, I tanned myself
all afternoon on coastal sands.
A shelter volunteer, I gave a new friend my fleece jacket
as she departed in October for the streets.
In glowing February sunlight, I pulled an earmuffed toddler
on his red sled through slush.

Newly married, I carried my trousseau in
five worn boxes through the April downpour.
In the garden, on a breezy summer morning, we stepped
across stones barefoot in the murky lily pad pond.
Walking in autumn, we kicked crackling leaves,
watching them float through air.
After his death, at winter's end, I found his old slippers
under the bed. I placed them neatly in the closet.
Summer, I warmed my dying mother with Nonna's old blanket.

Now, thinking about life after my death, the children in
the schoolyard next-door will play kick the can, and
my homemaker-neighbor will build birdhouses in her garden.
They will create their memories, little and big,
claiming the seasons as their own.

this summer evening
strolling neighborhood streets
i pick up my swollen feet
and run through the sprinklers
into my youth

rain in late august . . .
tinkle of the ice cream truck
long into sunset

nostalgic
with fountain pens and ink
in the drawer. . .
will my friends indulge me
by reading penned letters

wielding a duster
i hum to a music box
in my memory
wondering how much
of this dust is me

strolling a city
i frequented
in my prime,
the fog
obscures me

on a train
to my childhood home
following the moon

on a crisp autumn day
returning to my hometown
i walk to my old school
standing wistful
at the football field's fence

returning to my hometown . . .
the church
i left behind

my school chum . . .
still smiling ingenuously
at fifty-nine

my childhood home . . .
on the outside
looking in

in the closet
of my childhood home
i find a shoe box
where i buried my doll
with a broken neck

aging . . .
getting the freckles
i wanted in childhood

selling the home
of my childhood,
i walk into her closet
finding the shoes
i wobbled in

selling the home
of my childhood,
cleaning every speck
of dust
before i disappear

carnival music . . .
the round and round
of my hometown

my old school . . .
stillness of the
merry-go-round

after selling the home
of my childhood
i step into the taxi
bound for the airport
without a final glance

moving from the coast
to the heartland
i wake in the morning
to the calm of the lake
seeking the pounding waves

2 ~ Peace

Many people feel they don't have time for moments of peace with a job and family responsibilities. There is no quiet place at work or at home where they can sit in silence for a few minutes, and close their eyes without interruption. I can remember feeling this way when I was a caregiver to my bedridden mother. I could only experience a moment of peace when I went downstairs to the basement to sort laundry.

However, sometimes before falling asleep at night, I would take a few minutes, while sitting up in bed, to read a few haiku, one of the poetic forms in this book that I had discovered by accident in reading a reference book. When I didn't even have time for this, I would just take a few deep breaths to collect myself before falling asleep.

During another time in my life, I worked in an office without windows. I only had a half-hour lunch break and took it at my desk. During this break, I would sometimes take ten minutes to "hear" and "see" peace. I'd imagine hearing crickets sing or listening to a robin chirp. Or, I'd visualize flying a kite on the ocean shore or watching a hummingbird float through the air.

If you are lucky enough to spare a half-hour in your day, you can perhaps walk outside, sit on a bench, feel the wind touch you, watch falling leaves, blades of grass blowing in the wind, or a butterfly land on blossoms.

Why focus on nature? When I was younger, I didn't often stop to notice nature's beauty and peacefulness. Nature is uplifting.

Writing about peaceful scenes sustains us. Even when the weather is inclement, we can mentally transport ourselves to a peaceful place in nature. This diversion is worth the time.

reminding myself
to live in the present
i remove my watch
freeing my moments
into rippling air

lights out . . .
i see
silence

Between Sunrise and Midnight

Alone at home on a rainy day,
I silence clamoring machines
and dream from my window.

In my garden, an oriole flutters
above a potpourri of color.
I lose myself in lavender petals,
perfume of red freesia,
pink honeysuckle.

A turquoise butterfly fans
its black-speckled wings,
settling on yellow iris.
I savor raspberries,
inhale rosemary.

I walk unencumbered
through nearby woods
where trilliums refuse to hide.

Breeze brushes my forehead.
Crickets chant echoes from
my eardrums to heartbeats.

Beneath black sky, shadows
of pines whisper their scent
and watch over me.

Solitary Thoughts

A slow afternoon,
I walk past river pines
and bowing poplars,
crinkling leaves
on hard earth.

Sun touches cumulus clouds
glinting amber.
In and out of shadows,
I trail a schoolboy with
knapsack full of autumn.

My worn loafers veer off
the even path.
Buried in wildflowers,
I meditate in whirring wind,
invisible.

Muffled cries of crows
traveling eastward
become silent.
I settle in distant woods
laden with winter.

Beyond

Morning settles in, cleansing the sky.
Walking on the pebbled path
to the garden, my eyes rise from
dangling maple leaves to sunlight.

Sitting on Father's old pine bench,
I watch breeze brush the blades of grass.
Pink tulips, orange zinnias, and
lavender lean and whisper,

edge into my meditations,
lifting me deep into summer's breath.
Moments dissipate into caresses
on my forehead.

In a blink, my garden disappears,
sky unfolds. I reach into blue,
spinning, spinning away
to the hum of wings.

a stranger
in this bustling city
i retire at day's end
to the garden rooftop
beside the lotus pond

tai chi . . .
their movements
gentle the breeze

on my bookshelf
seeking *Think and Grow Rich* . . .
finding *Walden*

pulling her
into sunlight
on my old sled

at the portal
pausing in stillness
snowflakes grace her hair

in bitter cold
crossing the city bridge
over murky water
i see at a distance
the glistening mountain

new year's eve . . .
emptying the last
of the garbage

Wandering

After dreaming in color
through the night,
morning settles over the house
with my spaniel's sigh.

I rise, walk to the garden,
kneel on deep grass,
speaking softly to my violets.

Breeze carries a butterfly,
green, yellow, and blue,
over white rose petals.

A silver kite lifts
a neighbor boy into summer
across the creek and
singing stones.

Hearing chit-chat
of nameless birds,
my eyes open wide
to blossoming sun.

I wander in the brush strokes
of pastel sky
to the temple bells.

3 ~ Creatures

Creatures are our psychic companions. We marvel at sparrows flying in flocks like specks in the sky and goldfish navigating a small space in their bowl. We stare back into the eyes of a deer in the road and experience its soul. We hear the owl hoot, a cat purr, a dog sigh. The sight and sound of animals is often soothing. When we pause for thought, we realize that life, in any form, small or big, is wondrous.

Contemplating the habits of creatures is a diversion. We listen to the way they communicate with us and with other creatures. In writing about their place in our environment, we realize our gratitude for the gifts we have, and how humans are able to communicate on a higher level with language.

Do you remember your rabbit or hamster from childhood? They gave you hours of fascination, you learned to care for them, and they were friends. It's fun to write a poem about them.

As adults, we are appreciative of the many decades that we, in comparison to animals, are given on earth. Further, our dogs and cats teach us about basic tenets of living: love, loyalty, and acceptance. Of course, they amuse us— our dogs playing frisbee with us and our cats pawing a ping pong ball. Describing their antics in a poem provides relaxation.

When we lose a pet, writing about our grief and the things we miss about them, is a healing exercise. It is also a lasting tribute to our special friend who was, and will remain, a dear family member.

The Old Neighbor's Cat

Anna lounges in a tattered housecoat
in her tumbledown cottage,
furniture wobbly and scratched.

The mantel is bare, except for
a portrait of simple Albert,
her late husband, still smiling.

Despite scant belongings, Anna has
Augusta, her psychic companion,
with eyes of Prussian blue
and a diamond collar.

Head up, meowing,
and legs stretched,
Augusta, at once seraphic
and bewitching, stares at me.

Fiery-eyed, she leaps from
her armchair towards me,
sleek white, swaggering
as if on a runway.

I run my fingers back and
forth through her fur.
Hearing Anna's sweet talk,
she departs, returning to grace the chair.

Anna strokes her back, scratches
her head, and rubs her chin.
Soul of the cottage, Augusta purrs
herself to sleep, pawing the air.

Anna puts her finger to her lips, whispers
that her cat dreams of catching a mouse.
A breeze from the open window
gentles Augusta into the still of dusk.

in the red wagon
my brother and i bring home
our stiff cat

in the bare park
on a cold spring day
the pond thaws
as i listen intently
for the frog's return

my life upside down . . .
awaking to a fly
on the ceiling

after his death . . .
i sit in the tree house
listening to the owl

meal for a shut-in . . .
a mutt with cataracts
greets me on the porch

our dog's death . . .
her leash hangs next to
the children's coats

after his death
the doghouse empty
by starlight

after my dog's death
the breeze in the field
carries her bark

shut-in's bungalow . . .
on the window sill
a cat suns itself

in morning rush hour
a deer traverses
the lampposts
minutes from the crush
of the metropolis

from the open window
woodpecker . . .
punctuates my haiku

4 ~ People

We can't live in a vacuum for long, even though sometimes we feel like being alone. We all have a lot of obligations to ourselves and to others. We need some human contact to survive, even if just by technology or phone.

We notice others around us, and the good and bad in people. We become aware of the human condition, when we notice those less fortunate: the homeless, disabled, and immigrants adapting to a new country, job, and different customs. It's true that there are always people less fortunate than ourselves, no matter how many hard times we endure. Compassion for others is healing, because we stop focusing so much on ourselves.

In writing about strangers who cross our paths on the street and in public places, we often realize our human foibles. Writing about these weaknesses can be fun and humorous. Observing strangers often makes us smile.

Further, in writing about the joy of children in our lives, we relive what we were like as children. Writing about this, too, is a delightful exercise.

We all have the same hopes and fears. Writing poetry about the human condition is a release. When we read and write about people, we come to better understand ourselves. We realize that we aren't alone in our outlook on life and that we share the same struggles.

Homeless

snow flurries
he bundles
his bed

fading
into winter
his words

arctic winds
he walks past
the shelter

core of the city
he languishes
in twilight

fog blankets
the downtown bridge . . .
he vanishes

Seasons of The Homeless

sails in the breeze . . .
he pauses
at lakefront

driving home
i glimpse the full moon . . .
he pushes a shopping cart

walking to work
scattered leaves in my path . . .
their hollow eyes

frost on the park bench
he blankets himself
with a newspaper

biting wind
drifting snow
she sleeps on a pew

Foreigner

He arrives in his fifties
from his native land
living unknown.

Soft gray eyes, a calm smile,
voice cadenced
approaching a spring song.

A humble man,
wearing ill-fitted,
pressed pants and shirt,

he speaks of friendship
with undiscovered painters,
leaving behind war

to cross stiff winds at sea.
At times, he bows his head
in the grainy air,

sitting on driftwood.
August sunlight illuminates
his transparent hands.

He looks up and glimpses
a gull's wing tilting
at ocean's edge,

miles above his head.
He tells me today is
the best of yesterday,

something to remember
in twilight skies when
winds are with him.

november election . . .
fog masks
the candidate's smile

election day . . .
voters brave the winds
of pollsters

2016 election . . .
red states
trump the blue

at the thrift shop
a young man tries on
my father's shoes

Too Close for Comfort

sultry day . . .
motorist with tattoos
gives me directions

walking through the zoo
i keep my problems
in proportion

beyond, at the psychic fair
getting a reading
on the psychics

respite at the greasy spoon . . .
a man relishes
his promotion

café next door . . .
caught in the firing line
of the poetry slam

multi-lingual . . .
in my native tongue
i falter again

commuter train . . .
the clickety-clack
of foreign tongues

day's end . . .
cleaning women on the bus
speak their mother tongue

at the greasy spoon . . .
he rehashes
his divorce

at the diner
she serves us carbs and fats
with her life story

snowdrifts . . .
at the greasy spoon
he shovels mashed potatoes

neighbors drinking wine
on my terrace . . .
many shapes of vine leaves

on the park bench
remembering her fancy
a butterfly flits
from black-eyed susans
to patches of blue asters

standing near the poplar
i tell the neighbor's child
i do not know
how long it must grow
before touching the sky

road between cornfields . . .
old amish couple's buggy
long into sunset

pilgrimage
to the church
rummage sale

mother's day . . .
we talk again
in unison

table for one . . .
the bush mars
my view

the man
wearing worn shoes
asks me for the dance

"Season's Greetings" . . .
braggart's annual letter
fuels the yule log

class reunion . . .
i recognize
his swagger

clouds move in . . .
rainy-day neighbor
waves from a distance

meeting the new neighbor . . .
a mole tunnels
through my yard

weeding again . . .
the garter snake
the new neighbor

flat streets
of a midwestern town . . .
idle talk

searching my pocket . . .
only a soiled bill
for the blind man

shelter volunteer . . .
the teenager says goodbye
in my old wool coat

outside the café . . .
the blend
of homeless

at our thanksgiving table
i say grace, mindful of
the young man in the park
cocooned from hunger
face buried in his knees

blowing snow . . .
homeless man shivers
in tenor

homeless man
settles
on a corner

wind blows
through the cocoon
of a homeless man

waiting for the train
in evening snowfall . . .
homeless man's roar

hail clinks
the bridge railing
before the homeless man

Walking in Shadows

Phantoms haunt her.
She wavers in wind
past scattered houses
with chimneys puffing
wisps of smoke.
She crosses faded parkways
with tumbling twigs,
hollow leaves and
shadows of squirrels.
Wandering on slopes
past lifeless figures
and trams reduced to wires,
she descends into fog
on a narrowing passage.

The Homeless

Fog blankets the wooded hills,
distant city lights.
Autumn rain begins to fall,
thumping my bay window.

Yesterday, a man cloaked
in a garbage bag, walked
in the downpour past
windows of mannequins
handsomely attired.

Arctic nights ahead,
he will drift lightly shod
through blemished boulevards,
pelted by sleet.

Winds obscuring his worn face,
he will totter and vanish
on a bleak bridge
under invisible skies.

I leave the window now,
retiring to my room's pastels,
colors of spring solace and
of dahlias and primroses
to bloom in my garden.

In the still, my thoughts
turn to gray again.
I will rise at dawn, rushing
downtown in leather boots,
crushing shriveled leaves.

In my path, I will meet
another lost man with
lifeless gait and hollow gaze,
and walk in his dust.

slippery walkway . . .
a man with dark eyes offers
to steady my gait

car wash tunnel . . .
making resolutions
for the new year

approaching
the clerk
"next window"

express lane . . .
held up by
the teller

sultry day . . .
in line at the drive-thru
for a fry

moscow supermarket . . .
american greets the cashier
with a smile

5 ~ Work

So much of our lives revolve around work and dealing with the challenges of getting along with bosses, co-workers, and clients. Whenever my friends speak of problems with people connected with their workplace, I am sympathetic. We all experience similar situations. I tell them to write about work in their daily journal or to write a humorous poem about their general experiences. (These pieces shouldn't be for publication or be posted on social media, as they may defame or embarrass someone, and could also lead to your termination.)

Many people who write poetry as a hobby, find that this helps them achieve work-life balance. Some tell me they don't always feel their jobs allow them to be creative, so poetry is an outlet.

Even some medical schools publish literary journals, encouraging doctors to practice writing creatively. It is not only viewed as an outlet for doctors, but it spurs compassion for their patients and their feelings.

snowdrifts . . .
quitting my job to write
paper piled before me

stack of dirty dishes . . .
drizzle draws me
to the window

Another Draft

Forty-eighth or fiftieth?
I lose track again.
Scraps of scribbling
scattered, far-flung
behind the toaster
beneath the bedboard.

One moment, wordless,
next, wordful—
pummeled by an avalanche.
Buried under divisive devices
beneath the desk,
I choke on alliteration,
assonance, onomatopoeia,
hyperbole.

Creeping, crawling,
trolling, drawling,
hacking up restless syllables
parched to the tongue
too garbled to slide
onto smudged paper.

On my knees,
breath spent,
I open the window
for a few whiffs.
Through pine-scented sky,
hearing a warbler's refrain,
I crumple and pitch
my stale gibberish.

Seizing the Day

"Carpe Diem," they tell this simple bard.
These words confound me to my troubled core.
Housekeep and cook until I'm ninety-four.
I chop the beans, mash peas, and slice the lard,
and can the fruits until my palms are hard.
I dust and mop, such tasks that I abhor.
Sometimes I ask my mom, "What is life for?"
Can't pause to dream or shed my lonely guard.

Can I find hope this new day of the year?
I yearn to write my verses by the sea,
to hear the crickets sing from woods and fronds,
and lie beneath the moon to drink dark beer.
I'll learn to laugh once more to set me free
and find some special friends to form new bonds.

tears of the fireman
wash the soot
from his cheeks

      glazed snow on the steps . . .
      sliding a crisp bill
      into the mailman's envelope

            at the mailbox
            the frigid air
            nips my fingers
            reading the editor's
            snippy letter

The Will to Write

If I could write a sonnet just for me,
I would not fuss with complicated form
as many poets do that are forlorn.
I'd write, eat tarts, *gateaux*, and sip white tea.
In my imagination, I would flee
to homespun heartland where my kin were born
with fields and rows of oats, black beans and corn,
providing peace, abundant love, and glee.

I leave my house to roam where air is pure,
and find myself alone in silent woods,
inspired by the imagistic scene.
Hark All Artistes, the grandest ones for sure!
Like you, I have the will, the means, the goods,
my creativity is very keen.

runner in training . . .
feet pounding pavement
eyes fixed on the stars

end to the weekend . . .
the steam rises
pressing my white shirt

commuter train ride . . .
day breaks at
the terminal

lackadaisical boss . . .
his vocation
a vacation

Finding Peace

I write reports each day until I'm beat.
Complaints from my boss always bring me down,
nightly, I board the last bus from downtown,
can't find a seat to rest my swollen feet.
My hair's a mop, my skirt has lost its pleat.
Distrustful of riders, I stare and frown,
beside a man wearing a brooch with gown.
I wave my purse to fan the humid heat.

Yet, proud to own a home with funds for bills,
lacking lust for prestige that swells the head.
From my cottage, I'm soothed by sounds of rain.
When I read news about my country's ills,
homeless in tents, senseless wars and the dead,
I am grateful for a life with no pain.

golf with the boss . . .
my intern
overshadows me

once again this week
my boss belittles me
finding new words

smog in the forecast . . .
the boss delivers
a memo

from just warming my chair
to the hot seat—
he discovers my tweets

a certain relief
after meeting with the boss—
"you're fired"

dusk . . .
on the express train
motionless faces

6 ~ The Heart

We all seek love and acceptance. When we have them in our lives, it is a joyful experience to write about them. There are many kinds of love, not just between partners. Often there is the love of family and nurturing friends, and the love that comes with our beliefs in a higher form.

Love is an anchor, and it motivates us to self-discover, to do better in life, be kinder people, and even to get rid of our negative thoughts and bad habits. Love gives us the strength and self-confidence to tackle problems.

When we encounter rough spots in our relationships with others or people in our lives move on, writing about these can be healing. And, when a significant person in your life dies, writing about your grief is helpful, too. You can celebrate his/her life in a poem. And, at some point, in the near or far future, you look back on your writings and realize that you are a survivor. This has got to count for something. Resilience isn't just satisfying, but quite an accomplishment.

Writing about love's hurts will reveal to us how we've changed, have more wisdom, are able to put everything into perspective, and accept the challenges we are dealt in life.

Further, when hurts about severed relationships are written about in a humorous, exaggerated way—as we sometimes choose to do long after the loss—we're able to prove to ourselves that we are moving forward to a new chapter.

second time around
at the justice of the peace
wearing sensible shoes

second time around . . .
carrying my trousseau
in cardboard boxes

at sunset
sitting on a log
beside the ocean
his final words surface
with the crashing wave

alone on the road
by moonglow
stars illuminate stillness . . .
looking upward i see you
sharing my path

after his death . . .
finding old slippers
under the bed

grieving his death . . .
in the garden
i waltz in moonlight

in my grief
painting the red tulips
with a tinge of black

one visit
in twenty years . . .
one time left to see her

still waiting
for an apology . . .
on my walking route
passing a garden
of forget-me-nots

waking alone . . .
the tapping of
soggy snowflakes

grandfather . . .
the well
in his eyes

returning home . . .
the mist in my eyes
the well in mother's

my old mother tends daisies
telling stories about
my childhood

after mother's death . . .
finding my baby locks
in her box of jewels

newly married . . .
in a cabin
close to the clouds

moonlit sky . . .
following his footprints
in sand

summer wind
on the hilltop . . .
your caress

autumn evening . . .
walking a path of red and gold
to our cottage

at the table
his silence . . .
i stir my stew

distancing myself
from his biting words
i walk under dark sky
with misty eyes
breathing in salt air

his departure . . .
rain pummels
my yellow roses

an ocean apart . . .
past midnight
sleet sheets my window

moons of jupiter . . .
the distance of
his crimson heart

The Non-Event

CITY SWELTERS—
same headline, four days,
ninety-nine degrees,
ninety-five percent humidity.
Sun glints through smog.

In the evening, I drench
the rhododendrons and soak
the brown, brittle grass
flattened by footprints.
Ants swarm in cracks on the patio.

The neighbor's load of bricks
on a disabled Mack truck
mars my view. Telephone lines trap
my "Celebrate 60" balloon.
No one calls.

On the porch, I braid my hair
with yellow hibiscus and await
my old flame's return,
drinking spiked pink punch.
My cheeks droop to my jaws.

He arrives disheveled an hour late,
handing me a withered lily
picked at my garden's entrance.
Too old to care, I empty my thoughts
and melt into molecules.

moonlight . . .
he croons to me
out of tune

ice glazes the window . . .
our forks clinking
out of sync

his departure . . .
rain with snow splatters
on the window

An Acrostic

Plodding through withered leaves, I think of you,
Recalling the rhyme, *Liar Liar Pants On Fire.*
Endearment departed, I imagine you decrepit and
Vexed, haggard with white wisps and whiskers.
Ashen eyes simmer in your sallow face,
Riddled with raging wrinkles and pocks.
I didn't realize your insidious flaw until I saw
Curious shadows on a sultry September night.
All summer long, you swaggered in white pants,
Told white lies, wrote love letters with vacuous verse.
Over the cherry blossom hill, you recited Wordsworth.
Romping in sun, heat dissipated as we reached the decline.

7 ~ Seasons' Potpourri

We see beauty in the natural world. The seasons are something that we can count on to reappear, besides the sunrise and sunset. Many of us experience the warmth of spring sun, summer breeze, the reds and golds of autumn, and fresh drifts of snow.

The seasons provide us with hope and faith that things will work out, and that with their passing, time will heal our troubles. The changing of seasons brings us continuity in life, as it's expected. This is one of the things that anchors us.

We also know of the cruel forces in the environment that the seasons bring, such as hurricanes, earthquakes, tornados, flooding, and extreme heat or cold. Some experience deaths of loved ones attributed to these, or the loss of homes and irreplaceable possessions, such as photos and memorabilia. If we don't experience these ourselves, we see the devastation in the media. When we do, we have difficulty reconciling ourselves to the violence in our natural world, despite that it provides so many of us with solace and peace.

Some are forced to accept the good and bad in the natural world, just as we experience the good and bad in people. Dualities are part of our existence. In tragic times, we especially recognize the good in neighbors, strangers, family, and friends who lift us up.

Whether or not we experience natural disasters, we see the resilience of humans and eventual restoration of hope and calm.

Just Me and the Sun

A pelican burrows in deepening blue,
I nest in sand beside a rock
in a cove of swollen sun.

Bronzing to my core,
I ripen in salty sunglow.
Steaming heat reddens my hair,

soothes my eyelids,
and penetrates my cells.
My mind surfs pipe dreams

of riding wayward waves
in a funnel of rays,
discovering gold coins

in a bottle swept ashore,
and sailing far-flung oceans
in hot winds

with thoughts of my thoughts
drifting to sky's end.

Waste Not Summer

Scentless, can't shake this cold,
smell mown grass, nor
rose petals in the birdbath.
My violets and basil
lost in a fog.

Pocketful of tissues,
I stop for each sneeze,
clearing my cloudy head.
Misty cells evaporate
one by one.

Waste not a summer afternoon!

I dimple a peach that
soothes my worn gullet.

I touch the sun
on my spaniel's fur,

photograph a path of maples
on wavy hills.
The imposing oak supports
a lanky boy swinging
by his hands and wailing.

From the ginkgo,
jay bird's jeers and
wren's refrain.

At a distant park,
Little League cheers
spiral to the horizon.

Grand sun, long in setting . . .

ginko walk . . .
all the shades
of a haijin's words

september morning . . .
yellow jackets awash
in fresh-fallen pears

beside the eastern cottonwood
trembling in fall wind
a hunched farmer

closing my eyes
to feel
thunder's boom

rising at dawn
to autumn showers
i move to the armchair
in my faded robe
drifting off again

after the earthquake
wisteria flourishes
along the cracked wall

spring rain again . . .
winds blow silver
in sunlight

Autumn

at the window
watching
leaves rustle

after reading
the morning newspaper
i step out into gray

strolling the city
i frequented in my prime
fog obscures me

in the park
pine needles scent
the drizzle

fog lifts . . .
how lush
the downpour

The Sun Over Lake Michigan

Wind strokes us,
a gull cries, tilting
at lake's edge.

On a wayward afternoon,
oars measured like wings,
we sail in tandem over

the lull of ripples,
deepening blue.
Evergreens steady us
from a distance.

Ashore, walking in down boots,
I unspool my memories
of his breezy smile.

Branches, scented yesterday
with cherry blossoms, are
stripped bare.

Sunlight sails over
arctic waves,
piercing the ice ledge.

Sunbeams change course,
soften my stiff face,
awaken my dark eyes.
I melt into winter.

deep in the old growth
a downy woodpecker drums
to the warbler's trill

beyond
old growth . . .
sky

on the path
cherry blossoms in the breeze
gentle me

spring again . . .
awakening to the hum
of a tractor

hot dogs at the park . . .
the boy relishes
his home run

tornado warning . . .
i hear stillness descend
upon our farmstead

my first midwest winter . . .
working the snowblower
for a snowfall's inch

drifting snow . . .
tomatoes on the sill
ripen for salsa

Peaks

Peaks
Distant, untouched
Glistening, imposing, rising
They slice emerging clouds
Sovereigns

at the park . . .
winter grounds
the seesaw

sleet at nightfall . . .
he cloaks himself
in a garbage bag

8 ~ Solitude

Often, people think of solitude as a bad thing, equating it with confinement, such as illness, or even separation and loneliness. They feel solitude is a punishment, for example, viewing it as indicative of a "failure" after a broken relationship.

However, for some of us, solitude isn't a time of sadness or dark thoughts. Rather, it's a good thing when it provides us space to think, heal, and even write about our feelings, including our hurts.

Sometimes, solitude involves being homebound because of a drenching rainstorm or bone-chilling snowstorm. Often, writers do their best work during this time, just as artists and musicians do. We don't have the distractions of errands.

Your home can be a mystical place, a temple where you can meditate, be alone with your thoughts, or listen to soft music. You can sit beside the fireplace in winter.

For many, solitude doesn't necessarily mean being indoors, as we can find it in nature when we are without other people around. This can be an awesome experience.

I was born and raised in a beautiful part of the United States, the Pacific Northwest. I never fully appreciated the rivers, forests, mountains, and ocean until I was middle-aged. Then, I decided to write about them. I began seeing nature's majesty and wonder, and humans as being only a small part of the earth. When you are alone in nature, the sights and sounds are more pronounced.

Solitude is often a sanctuary. It gives us the time to wonder and discover our greatest thoughts. We are all poets and philosophers in our own way, but we need quiet to ponder.

Shades of Summer

Homebound, looking out
onto snowdrifts,
I unspool July.

The cardinal blazes in flight.
A scarlet butterfly, dappled white,
claims a yellow crocus.

I unravel raspberries
from a gnarled vine,
savoring seeds.

When twilight casts
a shadow,
the breeze strokes me.

In deepening green,
where roses refuse to hide,
the crickets' chant echoes
from ear to soul.

Into the Day

Heat fills the night,
gnats fester at the window screen
in jet black air.

I shut the metal blinds,
turn out the lights,
climb into bed.

Far from home,
darkening thoughts
bottled on the nightstand
haunt me.

Still awake an hour later,
I turn full circle,
push back the sheet
and move to an armchair.

Breathing long into
deepening humidity,
I drift through tangles
of blurry brown and disappear.

My eyes open to
arrows of dawn,
a fragmented life
through slats.

Tugging at the blinds
coated with dust, I lift and
release gloom.

Magnolia branches
graze the window.
I crack it open to
lemon-scented breeze.

Searching the stillness
of pastel sky, day rises
once more into focus.

Respite

White moon from my window,
sun-dried sheets, scented
with cedar and fir.
I lapse into a dream,
calls of a loon.
Branches bend on banks
of a runaway river,
clusters of evergreens,
cranes in deepening brown.
Night-walking the winding trail,
I spiral in wind through
a blaze of copper leaves
until gray wakes me to
the weight of a new day.

Ode to Shade

Soothe me, after months
of wasting sun.
Freshen my face.

Let me walk under
maple trees shedding
weightless crimson and gold.

Take me to childhood,
shuffling through leaves
of copper beech trees.

Sit with me on a hill
under poplar spires,
breezing beneath pale sky
flecked with sparrows.

Show me secret places in
a sanctuary touched by trillium.
Let my thoughts stream
with clarity and answers.

Share your quietude while
I breathe zephyrs of pine
before blizzards efface me.

My Routine

I wake to loose threads
dangling in my head.
From the bay window,

barely visible limbs of
a solitary poplar fan the air.
A train rumbles through the blur.

In my prairie town,
coffee percolates
black and gray moments.

I walk out into the chill
stumbling through twigs
and crusty leaves.

Through the maze of day,
I touch shoulders with tall shadows,
hear invisible robins.

With the maple leaves,
traffic lights change from
green to yellow to red.

Home at night,
I destroy pesky cobwebs
with my feather duster,

settle into my armchair.
Beating time in waning lamplight
to folk songs playing

in my childhood,
I drift into another dawn.

Long Moments

In early autumn beneath a sky
of gulls, wings tilt into the rays.

A bumblebee takes its last flight
without a buzz.

On clattering stones in a stream,
I listen to myself step,
tap dance, pause, breathe.

With the calm calling,
I climb the nearby hill
where maple leaves invite me.

Air breathes softer.

In my wanderings,
the greenery changes to
a burst of yellow, orange, red.

Once more, I long to
touch fallen leaves.

I relish my life's short stay.

lonesome on the prairie
i end this winter day
watching a sunset
of deep pink and orange
lifting me into spring

after winter seclusion
i open my window
hearing the woodpecker's rapping
and the tapping of
my old neighbor's cane

after the opera . . .
listening to
the downpour

living alone . . .
recognizing the footsteps
unknown neighbor

wooded hills . . .
the evening downpour
fogs distant city lights

lights out . . .
watching
thunderstorm

late evening
thunderstorms
pound my window
turning sadness
into guilt

The Dead of Autumn

Daylight overtakes her.
She rises and drifts outside
in a vapor of languor
vanishing into morning mist,
a hapless bird in fog
floating beneath
scraps of clouds.

She finds herself
in a garden
of motionless air
wilted daisies
faded cherry blossoms
and dewy ferns
beside pavement.

Remnants of life in
grayness of time.

Winter Solitude

Snowbound, melancholy.
I tell myself it's just winter.
The Christmas fir composts on the curb,
cheery holiday tunes and relatives gone.

Power outage, 14 degrees,
smelling smoke, pungent
from the hearth fire,
eating tepid stew.

Looking out my window,
a passerby with hunched shoulders
wraps his mittens around his arms,
hugging misery.

Three children admire their snowwoman
with tortilla chip hair,
circled by cosmic snowballs.

Snowdrifts breathe long.
Sparrows, absent from covered feeders,
no longer provide company.

Bundled in an old blanket with knit beanie,
snow pelts against the glass door,
blurring my eyes, off and on.

At sunset, purple tints snow.
Shadow of my birch forms a canvas
of feathery shoots.

Huffing wind wanes,
dusky sky empties into a lull.
I sense a kinship with
the red crossbill that whistles.

Black settles in.
My cedar with laden branches
glows by moonlight.

In candlelight, I contemplate warmth,
visualizing spring,
soulful walks in the old growth
under emerging blue.

alone at dusk . . .
drifting snow buries
my husband's footprints

awake at dawn
in my cold bed
i stare out the window
feeling the dark
of midnight

solitary walk
on new year's day . . .
my breaths dissipate into fog

after driving home
at midnight
shades of the blizzard
dart past my window
by the flickering lampposts

taking refuge
from torrential rain . . .
gray inside

after dinner
watching the tea kettle whistle
my bad day
dissipates
into the steam

on easter day
my home full of relatives
i seek quietude
slipping into my greenhouse
scented with lilies

                    mother's day. . .
                    my friends
                    celebrate

Loneliness

frigid air
on new year's day
one shade of white

drifts on the porch . . .
far from here
she has my name

buried in the yard
his red wagon
with rust

branches laden
with ice . . .
bedridden mother

shoveling again
the weight of
their words

winter deepens
grounding
the gate

alone at the table
after his scolding
i taste my salty chili
drinking in darkness
from the window

9 ~ Art

Viewing art is healing. When we notice the detail and beauty in an art piece, such as a painting, and write about what it conveys, we experience a sense of peace. Looking at a sculpture in a public square or in a park can relieve our stress, providing a sensory experience that can be restorative.

Some art is so powerful and meaningful to us, that we can connect with our feelings about our past, people we've known, places we've lived in or visited, or our dreams.

In recognizing the talent of artists, musicians, and other creative people, this gives us the ability to dream of our own creative potential. Many feel they aren't creative at all. But more times than not, they've never made creativity a hobby or a goal, so they haven't discovered their abilities. You may even start practicing a visual art that is often accessible, such as photography or calligraphy.

Whenever we view art, we enter into the lives and surroundings of those that created the piece. Art allows us to drift and dream, and leave our personal world of cares and concerns behind for at least a few moments.

At The Museum of Contemporary Art

Seeking quietude on a foggy day,
I visit the Museum to drift and dream,
with watercolors, collages, montages, and tapestries.
I happen upon worn scraps of metal, wire,
bits of broken glass, and splintered plastic.
Perhaps they are castaways culled from a hidden dumpster
in a deserted Chicago alley.

I visualize a sculptor in his cramped studio with a large window.
Under skies donning infinite grayness,
he watches languishing birds in autumn's breath.
Brittle poplar branches wave in whispering wind.
His eye glimpses fluttering scarlet and gold.
Inspired hands bend, chip, and polish refuse into delicate,
shining pieces, with soothing shades.

With agile fingers, his drab finds, a reflection of our gritty lives,
become graceful art, as if by metamorphosis.
He realizes sculptures of oddly-shaped people
and animals, almost unidentifiable,
yet bearing equilibrium and harmony.
In solitude, he finds lyricism
in trifles surrounding him.

The Pillar

Woman about town, fashionably plump, she didn't
work out at a gym nor play games at a power breakfast.
She was your matronly grandmother, a domestic specialist.
In her prime, God-fearing— faith, husband, children first.

Rotund, no-nonsense face, cropped hair, and
stocky legs firmly grounded in home life.
She didn't have street smarts, but her kids couldn't
fool her. She knew how to manage her life.
If she had baggage, no one realized it.

She always left the house with feathered hat
tipped to one side, gloves, and sensible shoes,
boundless hips rocking, generous arms swinging.

Wholesomely buxom, she bulged with pride
for family and community. Night out at
the VFW Post, she wore a ruffled dress,
accentuating her huggable build, and had a clutch purse.

She raised money for schools and orphans,
had four kids in six years, balanced a chubby baby
while vacuuming, cooked complete meals,
did piles of laundry, and ironed even the tiniest corners.

She didn't dream of finding herself.
Sitting beside her hearth with
the knitting circle was her me-time.

When she died, her reputation was bronzed
in neighbors' minds for living a solid life.
That recognition would have satisfied her.

**About *Standing Woman*, a bronze sculpture
by Fernando Botero.**

Timeout on the Prairie

Austere survivors of The Depression,
heartland settlers, pose for a portrait
in front of a farmhouse,
country church-like with steeple.

Balding farmer, sunken eyes,
circular glasses, clad in bib overalls
topped with a suit jacket.
In real life, the artist's dentist,
morose Dr. McKeeby,
no toothy smile.

Creases in his lower face match the lines
of the home's arched window.
His dirt-stained denims stitched
with a design of the hayfork's tines.
Beware: God-fearing, ill-natured man
armed with pitchfork.

At his side, sister of the clever artist
poses as the spinster-daughter.
Wholesome Nan avoids eye contact,
wearing a pained look. Hair tied back,
cameo brooch at her neck,
pressed apron over a black dress.

Oval-faced realists,
emblems of pride, perseverance,
and piety, too—
God bless those sullen souls!

**About *American Gothic*, a painting
by Grant Wood.**

Strangers

Along a boulevard,
they walk wet cobblestone,
garbed in grays and blacks.

There is rhythm to
umbrellas hooding
minds and souls.

Imposing dwellings and
gaslights tower above
unnoticed.

Some passersby look
straight ahead to a path
of fleeting moments.

Some, with heads bowed,
muse with measured steps.
In light and shadow,

rain effaces them.

**About *Paris Street: Rainy Day*, a painting
by Gustave Caillebotte.**

Intimate Moments

On Christmas Eve,
immersed in a painting,
my mind wanders.

A mother, wearing a generous robe,
holds her child on her lap,
cushioning the girl's flesh.
Her large hand wraps
around the child, gripping a towel
covering her lower body.

Bent over, with the other hand's
caressing motion, she washes
her daughter's tender foot
in an old metal bowl
next to a water pitcher
painted with dainty flowers.

The mother's attention to her child
of milk-white innocence moves me.
Wide cheeks, heads touching,
girl with brown hair, mother with black,
they resemble me and Mamma
as we once were.

If I'd had the daughter
I longed for, would she have
looked like me?

I would have treated her
with Mamma's care and affection.

**About *The Child's Bath*, a painting
by Mary Cassatt.**

museum concert . . .
i hear the watercolors
flow through the harp strings

from the ceiling
i hang my paper snowflake
sculpting the air

frigid air . . .
listening to the street flautist
i miss my train

music at the art center . . .
watercolors play upon
the pianist

The Crowd in Chicago's Grant Park

One hundred and six figures loom in the Park,
nameless, headless and armless,
each nine feet tall, eighteen hundred pounds.
We are lost in a wilderness of legs and feet.

Of bark-like mass, thick and wrinkled,
they are frozen in walking movement.
"Agora," the collection of hollow cast-iron,
cumbers and depresses cold earth.

Season after season, we mill around,
follow footprints, furrow and decay.
When winter comes, winds blur
and bury us in snow.

About *Agora*, a sculpture by Magdalena Abakanowicz.

Spiral of Love

Mother, cheek to cheek with
her son, embraces him,
an act of unconditional love
reflecting God's.

On her lap, the boy smiles
blissfully, eyes lift to sky,
his arms wrap around
her neck and back.

Mother's contemplative mood
gentles and heals us,
eyes cast downward,
humble as the Virgin Mary's.

Her legs in lotus position,
soft bare feet evoke the path on
the hard soil of our broken world.

In the swirl of modern life,
the free-spirited woman with
flowing hair, radiates peace

and caring on Mother Earth.
Together with her son's embrace,
a spiral of love.

**About *Compassion Moves a World*,
an outdoor sculpture by Julie Rotblatt-Amrany
in Highland Park, Illinois**

What's All the Roar?

Two museum guards, eight feet tall,
boast fangs and jowls,
capable of savaging
in one breath, one swallow.

Flanking the doors,
the bronze sculptures,
lionized as landmarks,
take us back to the battle
with unicorns for crowns.

In the urban wild, we pose for pictures
riding the jungle kings, at times
decorated with holiday wreaths
or helmets honoring sports teams.

A feline fanatic amid Chicago's roar,
I dream of creating art revered
as the beastly guards,
ferociously-treasured as

Stati's *Samson and the Lion*
and Delacroix's *Lion Hunt.*
I ride high, if only
for a few moments,
before touching ground.

**The lion sculptures by Edward Kemeys stand
at the entrance of The Art Institute of Chicago.
They "guard" the museum's pieces inside.**

Urban Pasture for The Divine Bovine

Whimsy in The Windy City, a cow
on the moove, elegantly hoofed.
Chi-cow-go amid skyscrapers,
where city dwellers discover
their prairie roots.

Endearing, docile face,
enduring body, eight feet long,
sculpted in bronze
on a crowded sidewalk.

Forget the mundane,
How Now, Brown Cow,
and the tale of Mrs. O'Leary's cow
that burned us down.

Matronly, but not ungainly,
an aura of grace with
prominent hip bones,
Mother Bovine, udderly nurturing.

A molded beauty, eyes etched
with city landmarks—the Picasso and
Water Tower—cosmopolitan cow.
She gleams in summer sun,
ogled by foreign tourists.

A woman climbs on her back,
flashing the peace sign for the camera.
We line the pavement, waiting
to stroke her body, trace her delicate ears,
un-cowed by her celebrity.

**About the bronze cow sculpture by Nathan Mason
in front of the Chicago Cultural Center.**

10 ~ *Wonder and Whimsy*

There are many ways we can lose ourselves in wonder and whimsy. We can, for example, experience nature, art, and relive childhood memories or a better time in our lives. We often lose ourselves in the child-like wonder of holidays and write about them. We can read today's horoscope, and even those of the past few days, to see if the predictions were on target, allowing us to wander in possibilities.

If you aspire to being a poet, let your mind daydream and see the world with a child's innocence. Wonder about the shapes and sizes of things around you. It can be fascinating to write about these things. Your imagination provides a great escape, and writing poetry is a good method of satisfying your curiosity.

Poetry is a safe place for our dreams. Write about what your heart desires. Make believe you could play with a former childhood friend. Who would you pick to play with and what game would you play?

Pretend you had a net to catch a favorite moment in your life. Which one would you chase after? Write a poem about it.

Make believe you discovered a secret tunnel. Write a poem about what was inside the tunnel and where it led you.

Personally, I love the whimsical activity of observing things in nature, and connecting what I see in it to what is happening in my personal life. As revealed in the haiku in this book, there is often a connection between an image in nature and how the poet is feeling. The grayness of the sky may also reflect the gray mood of the poet. Or, the twists and turns of the bonsai are akin to those in our own lives.

Japanese style-poems reflect the concept that people are one with nature.

In Japanese-style poems, we often see two seemingly unrelated images and find they are connected, when we pause to ponder the poet's thought process.

In senryu, a Japanese form that deals with human nature, we can see the humor in people around us—often in the connection between two seemingly unrelated images.

Further, poetry allows us to play with words—even create our own, or to play with rhyme. Limericks are a good example of wordplay and rhyme. I love the whimsy of poetry and the solace it brings to me for these reasons, too.

Daydreaming is fun. We can watch gulls, and wish that we, too, could fly. We can fly or soar in other ways, that is, figuratively, in dreaming of personal goals and aspirations. Write about your dreams.

A Speck in the Universe

Skylark sings in soft air.
Sun shifts, shines into my eyes,
morning settles over my lilies.

I sniff shimmers of summer.
Butterfly flits from black-eyed
Susan to blue aster.

Clematis touches cloudless sky.
King ostrich ferns, trumpet vines
vie for attention.

Sycamore reigns over weeping willow.
My shadow breathes in, out, vanishes.
I blush into green on the path.

Carpe Diem

In July, I lose myself in nature.
Under deep sky, I break in a new hammock.
Day moon rises between leafy poplars.
Somewhere in silence a songbird whistles.

I see rhythm in the hummingbird's whir.
A golden eagle glides with my thoughts.

Juicy plums hang onto the breeze.
A butterfly alights on limp rose petals.
Red dahlias in my rusty containers
vie for attention.

Quilled into grass, a robin's feather catches
my eye. I pull out my writer's pen and pad.

Inspired but lazy, I whistle off-key.
Minutes later, I nap the hours away.

I dream about a sweat-browed farmer
in a green barn, frantically shouting
to his old Holsteins as a twister
spirals them to Saturn.

I awaken to an ice cream truck's tinkling
tune and raindrops tapping my arm.

Hot wind turns cool,
ruffles my T-shirt and shorts,
pulling my hat off to fickle summer.
Day flatlines through ripples of air.

Games With My Tomboy Sister

She had leaves in her thick, cropped hair,
bruises under her raccoon eyes,
and scratches on her scrawny legs
from scaling the oak to the tree house.

She was my shadow, hopping
ahead of me with brittle bones.
I followed her tracks in dirt and dust.

Despite her slight build,
she was stronger than I,
pushing me high on my swing
so I could grab at clouds.

We stalked the neighbor boys
in the alley, camouflaged in the hedge.
We jumped out laughing, brandishing
our pocket knives, watching them flee.

When it rained, we played inside,
forgetting our boyish ways.
We dressed up Barbie, Ken, Midge
and Skipper, draining poor Dad's budget.

Summers at the beach, we searched
for sand dollars and seaweed
and built tunnels to Africa.

In our shared bed, under
Nonna's quilt, buried beneath
countless stars, we hid from spiders.

She was my breezy companion
to tell secrets and recite rhymes to,
yell and toss feather pillows at.

Carried by winds through childhood,
she was unknown to Dad and Mom.

Mother Earth

I'm a contrarian.
Wherever I find myself,
black and white often attract me
more than bright colors.

Alone under night sky,
I dream by day
under clouds.

First day of summer,
lilies bloom as the lizard
slithers on the porch.

Picking up pebbles
wet with tide, I discover
a sand dollar unmarred.

Ides of October,
the faint cry of a snow goose
calls to me near the wharf.

November rain,
charcoal-spotted leaves
pepper the grass
of a mountain church.

Snow buries my yard in February.
My eyes trace patterns of
bare oak branches etched in sky.

In spring mist, a blackbird
whistles at me and disappears.
Hail follows, salting the forest.

With freshly tilled soil, the rabbit scurries
around the barn. Inside, an old hen
takes shelter, flapping her wings.

Black beans, parsnip, cauliflower,
coconut, and coffee— the subtlety
and mood of monochromes.

Halloween

Still
pale moon
aromas
of cauldron brew.
Disguised as a ghost,
smoky-fog surrounds me.
Toothy jack-o-lanterns line
steep steps with skulls and skeletons
in the deepening dim of twilight.
A warty witch dangles from the warped fence.

evening flight . . .
turbulence
in stillness

reading
yesterday's paper . . .
my horoscope

tucked in bed
on a school night
he studies the stars

pruning
the bonsai . . .
my knotty life

four-leaf clover half brown

lush jogging route . . .
the parish priest greets me
in his red shorts

cynicystic

snowed in . . .
after the piña colada
dreaming in color

blank page
in my diary . . .
i search the clouds

intruder in my bedroom—
moon
with the wolf's howl

on my 55th birthday
watching the flight
of the hummingbird,
wishing i could float
through each day

on my way
to the polls
passing two scarecrows

postman arrives . . .
in my palm
i weigh the reply

reading my Boccaccio tales . . .
the parish priest waves
from his convertible

leaving the bank
with six figures
on the odometer

scarecrow
makes a statement
wearing my old tie dyes

The Edge

Months after you ditched me,
my head's still dizzy, my brain wires dangle.
"Haunted by delusions," my therapist says.
A mummy afoot enters my home,

walks up behind me, knocks at my skull.
Racing out the door, Godzilla stalks me
with god-awful rants.
Outrunning him on the beach,

I swim out to sea, swirling to
the depths of seething sea serpents.
Crimson fears savage me,
despair clots my blood.

Tangled in seaweed, my body surfaces.
Dazed, I wander in the salt fog of
the coastal range, attacked by a werewolf
with sparking fangs. Skeletonized,

I creak and crackle along crooked paths.
Near my tumbledown cottage
on the eroding bluff, my black shadow
dogs me, goading me over the edge.

Apothecary Ronald Kahn
awoke fatigued and pained at dawn.
He led a stressful life
splitting pills with a knife
until he OD'd and was gone.

The jock pumped up at the gym
shrinking beer belly with vim.
Broke his back with two-tons,
home in bed with no funds,
his harebrained jockettes dumped him.

Our belligerent boss Tonia Airy
demeaned us, her profanity scary.
Lying and cheating at her job
'til we mutinied, formed a mob—
disgraced, she committed hari-kari.

LuAnn's lover was a dandy
gifting her cologne and candy.
He left his witchy wife
to woo her without strife
later ditching her for Randy.

11 ~ The Spiritual

Have you heard your friends say that they aren't spiritual? Even if one isn't religious, all people are spiritual. As human beings, we are surrounded by nature and creation, and we marvel at the earth's wonders.

Even if people are half awake, they cannot help but be touched by the beauty around them at some point. It's safe to believe that there is at least a hint of spirituality in each of us.

Further, there is the question of an afterlife. Everyone ponders life after death, particularly when they lose a loved one. We look for signs that they are still among us. We look for their faces in the sky, the moon, or stars, hoping they are looking down on us and guiding us during our difficult times.

We wonder what will become of us when we die: eternal rest, heaven, hell, or reincarnation? Whether one believes that heaven and hell exist or are merely constructs, we sometimes wonder about reward or punishment after death. Perhaps you could write hopeful poetry about the afterlife, as you would dream it to be for you.

turbulent flight
i relax my sore eyes
bounce on clouds
dreaming of discovering
the mysteries of creation

Nearing Eternity

My heart throbs as I pull my red kite
streaming under morning blue
along the ocean shore.

Breathless, I stop. I gaze above, watching
gull's wings shimmer towards sky's end.

I marvel at the silence. I am.

I wonder, if in the afterlife, I'll move deeper
into the light beams, reunited with loved ones,
their spirits surrounding mine.

A chill distracts me.

Toting the kite, I walk back to the cottage,
drafting my last chapter.

before confession . . .
wood crackles
on the hearth

last one to confess . . .
hastening to leave church
before the priest's exit

after confession . . .
eating christmas fudge
from the monks

after the sermon . . .
in trouble again
with the almighty

Good Friday . . .
walking to confession
in worn shoes

in the confessional screening my words

leaving confession . . .
at the corner greasy spoon
flames rise from the grill

storefront church . . .
in my heart
i feel the drumbeat

caught in the firing line
of the corner evangelist—
no salvation

sweep of the tornado
through a churchyard . . .
yew trees crisscross

The Smoke

I open the mailbox to cumbersome bills.
For a few moments, I dream of enjoying riches—
a seaside villa, sunbathing on Brazilian sand,
indulging in mai tais and chocolate cigars.

Holy smokes! Don't be blinded, I tell myself.
I listen to the view: a gull's cry through a puffing cloud,
a robust robin's chirp on a sun-streaked maple,
gibberish of the neighbor-girl, up to her chin
in sunflowers, a hummingbird rippling through air.

I enter my sparse cottage, sit by the window.
Writing checks, I retrace numbers so they won't be
misread. Then, I burn incense, drift toward nirvana.

how small her room
in which she lies bedridden
but how vast the sky
filled with blue
awaiting her arrival

Afterlife

Calm
Silence.
I ascend,
spiraling to
the summit. Seabirds
glide to meet me, from sand
to sublimity, lost in
cantatas of rippling refrain.
Lilac, lilies, and pale peach roses
perfume the dust of a marigold haze.

12 ~ *Aging Illness Death*

Aging, illness, and death are preoccupations for many of us. How long will we live, and in what condition will we find ourselves in the future?

Hearing about someone in the news who has died in an accident, reinforces our thoughts about life's fragility and its random nature.

In childhood, we may have been struck by seeing our grandparents decline in health and die. In adulthood, we face the same with our aging or ill parents. Sometimes, we experience the deaths of our children, younger friends, siblings, or co-workers.

Writing about aging, illness, and death is often a necessity. If one is a caregiver or has been to her ill child or elder, or if one is a caregiver by career, writing about this experience is an outlet. I began writing about illness when I was a caregiver to my mother. When I was forty-eight years old, I wrote about my own aging, following the caregiving and death of my mother. Were it not for my feeling worn out as a caregiver, I may not have thought forty-eight was old.

When we grieve the death of someone close to us, we often don't want to burden our friends and relatives with our feelings. Writing about grief is an alternative.

In this book, there are many short, Japanese-style poems such as haiku, written about wisdom and healing, as the Introduction to this book reveals. Haiku is a powerful form for expressing one's emotions, particularly about illness and death. The style of haiku—usually one to three lines—reveals the poet's emotions stated in a matter-of-fact way. This understatement is something that makes one's words all the more powerful for those who read them.

For poets who prefer not to use haiku's matter-of-fact style, the forms of free verse or tanka, also in this book, may interest you. Tanka is discussed in the Introduction. It is a short, lyrical poem of five lines.

Whichever poetic styles appeal to you, be mindful that others won't judge you for revealing your innermost feelings. Evocative emotions are what poetry is about. Readers will understand and appreciate your candor and courage.

The Dust

I look at lingering fog
and crusty leaves.
Inside, another Sabbath

of housework begins,
a black apron
around my neck.

My worn hands dust the table.
One swipe with a rag
and white blackens.

Dust descends to the rug
like dandelion puffs drifting.
It hides in fibers.

Above the mantel, I remove
film from the mirror.
Behind loose strands of hair,

I stare at my aging self,
getting the freckles
I wanted in childhood.

The radio plays dissonant,
nameless sonatas
with sobbing violins.

I vacuum with Mother's Electrolux,
drowning out the requiem,
wondering how much of this dust is me.

fiftieth birthday . . .
in my flower bed
pulling weeds

after mother's illness
she takes her first steps
into autumn wind
leaning against me
both of us wavering

signal changes . . .
he gathers himself
with his cane

uncle's ninetieth year
i gather the figs
he planted

at dawn
her caregiver leaves
another arrives

after suffering
through illness alone
her family sends notice
of her memorial
celebration

childless . . .
looking at grandmother's face
in the mirror

my bedridden mother
wan and still
stares at the window
framing the cherry blossoms
she planted in her prime

summer heat . . .
with raw hands i bathe
my bedridden mother

this chilly evening
in late autumn
sitting at mother's bedside
i listen to the clanging
of the parlor's clock

i warm
mother's cold hands . . .
next life pending

mother's last breath . . .
my dog leaves us
alone

Spring Again

Mother died just moments ago. Hannah, the gentle black Labrador who lies at the foot of the bed, leaves the room. I turn and tell Margaret, Hannah's owner and Mother's close friend, that she is gone. There is no pulse. Margaret is somber, sitting at bedside with head bowed. She doesn't respond.

A minute later, as she stares at the wall, Margaret tells me this is the first time she has witnessed a death. We had expected Mother's passing for a few days now. Her breaths had gotten farther apart. I had been giving her doses of morphine, instructed by the hospice nurse.

It is the end to sixteen years of illness. I inhale once and exhale to allow myself to feel relief from exhaustion— emotional, physical, and mental.

Tired from standing over Mother, I sit down in a chair, looking at her body. Mother looks as if she struggled for her last breath, her upper lip raised and lopsided.

It is warm, the sky is blue, in mid-morning. In early May, it is usually overcast and rainy here. I feel a breeze through the open window that looks out onto the blooming cherry blossom tree Mother planted.

The phone rings, interrupting my thoughts. Margaret gets up and walks into the hall to answer it. She responds in a matter-of-fact tone to the caller: "She has died . . . yes . . . goodbye."

I ask about the caller. A telephone solicitor, Margaret says. I think to myself, she could have just told the stranger, "She's not in."

> once more
> the breeze
> gentles me

in autumn's chill
light shining through pale sky
i stand at the grave
with misty eyes
talking to mother

lingering with him . . .
i watch the wind scatter
his ashes

Autumn

I walk home in twilight's drizzle
through mud on a sunken trail.
Falling leaves bury others.

Old growth in the distance
dies with the day,
uprooted by bulldozers.

I follow a stranger's tracks along
a silhouette of pines,
hearing the call of a nuthatch.

On my porch, wood creaks
and slopes. My spaniel no longer
waits for me.

Inside, sitting across from chairs,
I eat on Mother's chipped china,
her pastel linen wrinkled and stained.

Skies clear, I leave the table,
moon follows me through the house.
Wind rushes through a row of
poplars showering leaves.

In the mirror, I trace creases
and pieces of myself,
recalling the nursery rhyme,

*There was an old woman
Lived under a hill,*
that repeats until
it lulls me to sleep.

Winter Dim

Gusts and ice pellets,
then slant of snow
blur the window,
attacking the hollow oak, once
cradling my childhood swing.

I wander for a few moments,
smell fresh-mown grass,
finger plum blossoms beneath
unblemished sky, and follow
bluebird song.

Yesterday, a straw hat for
covering my gray hair, hung
in the mud room. Today, as I rub
my arms, dry from itchy wool,
early dusk settles on the keyboard.

Unworn white lawn mitigates
black sky. Winds through the cedar
cease their swoosh, snowfall lightens.

The tea kettle blows fog.
As I rise, my knees jerk from
advancing age. I pass through
a spider thread, avoiding my old hound
who snores into tomorrow.

Sitting down for tea, I sip ennui,
and reach for a novel, popular during
my prime, in large print now.

forty-fifth reunion . . .
seniors
again

advancing age . . .
pine needles in the forest
soften the path

at the senior center . . .
he rocks
on the dance floor

Lost in Autumn

brown leaves . . .
we walk the path
to his log cabin

pausing
father asks
what month it is

twilight
the wind
dogs us

wooded hills . . .
rain fogs
distant city lights

taking refuge
from the downpour . . .
his dark walls

after listening
to arias
the torrents

lights out . . .
in his armchair
he watches thunder

closing his eyes
feeling
the boom

he retires . . .
gazing at the window's blur
he fades

her last days . . .
in the kitchen
filling jars with jam

mother's day . . .
wrapping the pink dress
for the funeral home

Nearing the End

On the dusty porch, overlooking a wall
of oaks, night overtakes him.
The roar upon the rails appears,
disappears before his creased face.

He no longer knows where the lake begins,
where the somber river ends.
A breeze grazes him.

His sunken eyes gaze at
the serene moon before it melts.
He sees stars crumble to
blackened bits in sky's hush.

He has specks of life left.
Through the open window,
he doesn't hear the pendulum
on the mantel beside photographs.

A familiar face, often distant
as Mercury, moves closer.
For a moment, her smile touches him
before it's lost in dimness.

Beneath the heavy boughs,
autumn's reds and yellows shrivel,
swept by curls of wind into dust.

The End

In his youth
in sprawling summer
he sailed the solitude,
open to winds and waves,
bronzed by sun.

As a man
he watched the sun
slowly die.
He walked a long corridor
under barren trees,
often losing his path.
In rustling wind
the path was thick
in withered leaves
and hollow leaves.

There is no horizon now,
no daylight.
Only a silent evening
on a deserted street,
dusted in white.
Only a motionless face
in a dim room,
dreams wilting
on the pillow.
In his eyes
winter.

walking at dusk
in blistering hail
and gnawing wind
his ravaging illness
accompanies me

in this season of decay
another year older
i watch brown leaves
turn to dust
in a wind's curl

blowing out his candles
grandfather's button
hangs by a thread

Uncle's Death

Maple leaf free-falls and
falls to frozen ground.
A crow caws.
Breeze slips through
window crevices.

On the oak dresser,
dust settles on a bent photo,
pocket comb, ship's clock.

From his metal-frame bed,
Uncle speaks haltingly,
melding patches of eighty-four
autumns with golds, wine reds,
brittle browns.

The clock tolls at half-hour.
He winds down into fog.

night of his death . . .
one star dims
for each dream

Grandfather's Death

arctic winds . . .
he tends the fire
from his armchair

winter deepens . . .
bedridden, he looks at
branches laden with ice

late April thaw
my hands warm
his limp feet

after his death
the dogwood he planted
blossoms again

ashes . . .
i scatter
his life

rising at dawn
i gaze at wrinkles and
spots in the mirror
mindful that i will turn
into dust after death

alone at home
in my waning years
i sit in the alcove
rocking my chair
to the rhythm of silence

easter morning . . .
i climb to the summit
scattering his ashes

news of his death
i stand shattered
at the window
gazing at ice jams
on the gray river

after mother's death
saving her gift
of parchment

gravestone
after gravestone
withered flowers

after his death . . .
they fill our table
with cold cuts

after his death
i walk to the frozen pond
in the park
where he used to sail
his toy boats

after mother's death . . .
a queen bee hovers
over my window sill

Excursion

Roses needn't be red, white or yellow.
I see purple in them, as in lilacs and orchids.

I take a few moments to sit in my room,
empty my mind of tiring tasks,
and taste the rose-scented rippling air
of my summers and winters.

In my twilight years, I discover the shades
of my decades, noticing deep colors.
Purple is in my moods, sorrowful or peaceful,

watching sunset's amethyst clouds
darken the roses or the butterfly's violet
wings skimming over regal petals.

I feel roses' moist buds, see the sound
of falling blossoms in sun and rain
during this short stay.

Appendices

Bibliography: Poetry Books & Anthologies
Recommended for Healing, Peace, or Diversion

Balistreri, Mary Jo. *Gathering the Harvest*. Shoreline, WA: Bellowing Ark Press, 2012.

_ _ _. *Still*. Athens, GA: Future Cycle Press, 2018.

Barks, Coleman, trans. *A Year with Rumi: Daily Readings*. San Francisco: HarperOne, 2006.

Beary, Roberta. *Deflection*. Lexington, KY: Accents Publishing, 2015.

_ _ _. *The Unworn Necklace*. Liverpool, England: Snapshot Press, 2007.

Bishop, Elizabeth. *The Complete Poems 1927-1979*. New York: Farrar, Straus and Giroux, 1983.

Collins, Billy. *Aimless Love: New and Selected Poems*. New York: Random House, 2014.

Dancy, Carolyn Coit, ed. *this world: Haiku Society of America Members' Anthology*. New York: Haiku Society of America, 2013.

Dickinson, Emily. *The Collected Poems of Emily Dickinson*. Overland Park, KS: Digireads Publishing, 2016.

Dotson, Jennifer, ed. *Coffee, Tea & Other Beverages*. Highland Park, IL: Highland Park Poetry, 2018.

_ _ _, ed. *Driving Cars*. Highland Park, IL: Highland Park Poetry, 2019.

Dunphy, John. *Old Soldiers Fading Away*. Columbus, OH: Pudding House Publications, 2006.

Epstein, Robert, ed. *All the Way Home: Aging in Haiku*. West Union, WV: Middle Island Press, 2019.

_ _ _. *Checkout Time is Soon: More Death Awareness Haiku*. West Union, WV: Middle Island Press, 2018.

_ _ _, ed. *Now This: Contemporary Poems of Beginnings, Renewals, and Firsts*. Shelbyville, KY: Wasteland Press, 2013.

_ _ _, ed. *The Sacred in Contemporary Haiku*. CreateSpace, 2014.

_ _ _, ed. *The Temple Bell Stops: Contemporary Poems of Grief, Loss and Change*. Baltimore: Modern English Tanka Press, 2012.

_ _ _, ed. *They Gave Us Life: Celebrating Mothers, Fathers & Others in Haiku*. West Union, WV: Middle Island Press, 2017.

Forrester, Stanford M., ed. *seed packets: an anthology of flower haiku.* Windsor, CT: bottle rockets press, 2010.

_ _ _. *smiling anyway: selected haiku and senryu.* Windsor, CT: bottle rockets press, 2019.

Fraticelli, Marco, and Claudia Coutu Radmore, eds. *Wordless: Haiku Canada 40 Years of Haiku.* Banff AB, Canada: Ekstasis Editions, 2017.

Frost, Robert. *Selected Poems of Robert Frost.* New York: Sterling, 2018.

Gorman, LeRoy, ed. *on down the road: Haiku Society of America Members' Anthology.* New York: Haiku Society of America, 2017.

Guest, Edgar A. *Collected Works of Edgar A. Guest.* Charleston, SC: BiblioLife, 2008.

Hall, Donald. *White Apples and the Taste of Stone: Selected Poems 1946-2006.* New York: Houghton Mifflin Company, 2006.

Harrison, Devin, and Mike Montreuil, eds. *at the water's edge: Haiku Canada Members' Anthology.* Carlton Place, ON, Canada: Haiku Canada, 2019.

Hass, Robert. *Human Wishes.* New York: Ecco Press, 1990.

Johnson, Caroline. *The Caregiver: Poems by Caroline Johnson.* Duluth, MN: Holy Cow Press!, 2018.

Kacian, Jim, ed. *big data: The Red Moon Anthology of English-Language Haiku.* Winchester, VA: Red Moon Press, 2015.

_ _ _, ed. *Carving Darkness: The Red Moon Anthology of English-Language Haiku.* Winchester, VA: Red Moon Press, 2012.

_ _ _, ed. *in a hole in the light: The Red Moon Anthology of English-Language Haiku.* Winchester, VA: Red Moon Press, 2019.

Kocher, Philomene, and Marco Fraticelli, eds. *far galaxy: Haiku Canada Members' Anthology.* Carlton Place, ON, Canada: Haiku Canada, 2018.

Kooser, Ted. *Kindest Regards: New and Selected Poems.* Port Townsend, WA: Copper Canyon Press, 2018.

_ _ _. *Sure Signs: New and Selected Poems.* Pittsburgh: University of Pittsburgh Press, 1980.

Kumin, Maxine. *Where I live: New & Selected Poems 1990-2010.* New York: W.W. Norton, 2011.

Laity, CJ, ed. *JOMP: Journal of Modern Poetry.* CreateSpace Independent Publishing Platform, 2012.

_ _ _, ed. *Poetry Cram: The Ultimate Chicago Poetry Anthology.* Chicago: ChicagoPoetry.com Press, 2012.

Lanoue, David G. *Write Like Issa: A Haiku How-To.* New Orleans: HaikuGuy.com, 2017.

Mason, Scott, ed. *sharing the sun: Haiku Society of America Members' Anthology.* New York: Haiku Society of America, 2010.

McClintock, Michael. *Meals at Midnight.* Baltimore: Modern English Tanka Press, 2008.

McDonald, Tanya, ed. *A Moment's Longing: Haiku Society of America Members' Anthology.* New York: Haiku Society of America, 2019.

Miller, Arlyn, and Susan Gundlach, eds. *in plein air: poems and drawings of the natural world.* Glencoe, IL: Poetic License Press, 2017.

Oliver, Mary. *Dream Work.* Boston: The Atlantic Monthly Press, 1986.

Parker, Dorothy. *Complete Poems.* New York: Penguin Classics, 2010.

Radice, William, ed. *Selected Poems of Rabindranath Tagore.* London: Penguin Classics, 2005.

Rozmus, Lidia, ed. *Climbing Mole Hill: An Anthology of Haiku and Haiga for the Republic of Mole Hill.* Evanston, IL: Deep North Press, 2015.

_ _ _, Joseph Kirschner and Charles Trumbull, eds. *A Travel-Worn Satchel: Haiku Society of America Members' Anthology.* Evanston, IL: Deep North Press, 2009.

Sandburg, Carl. *Honey and Salt.* New York: Harvest Books, 1967.

Shinder, Jason, ed. *The Poem I Turn To: Actors and Directors Present Poetry That Inspires Them.* Naperville, IL: Sourcebooks MediaFusion, 2008.

Stafford, William. *Even in Quiet Places.* Lewiston, ID: Confluence Press, 2010.

Strand, Mark. *The Continuous Life: Poems.* New York: Knopf, 1992.

Taylor, Richard Allen. *Armed and Luminous: poems by Richard Allen Taylor.* Charlotte, NC: Main Street Rag Publishing Company, 2016.

Wilbur, Richard. *Richard Wilbur: New and Collected Poems.* New York: Harcourt Brace Jovanovich, 1988.

The Author's Thoughts on Making Poetry Accessible

Charlotte Digregorio has spent her adult life as a writer and educator. She actively promotes the literary arts. The author received an official commendation from Illinois Governor Bruce Rauner in 2018 for her lifelong accomplishments in the literary arts, and her work to promote and advance the field by making it more visible to adults and students.

Digregorio says, "It's a habit for me to think about writing no matter what I'm doing, even when I wash my car. I host literary gatherings in my living room and poetry open mics, hold Board positions on writers' organizations, and organize national conferences." Digregorio has mentored dozens of aspiring writers in multiple genres who've become authors and taught others. "Mentoring is my passion and calling," she adds.

Among her activities to make the literary arts visible to the public, she holds solo exhibits for her illustrated poetry 'year round in the Midwest. Her poetry combines graphic art and photography, among other visual arts. These exhibits are in public/academic libraries, art galleries, corporate and park district buildings, hospitals, botanic gardens, and cafes. Her individual poems have appeared on public transit, in theatres, supermarkets, restaurants, wine shops, parks, nature and community centers, banks, and apparel stores.

"We must make poetry accessible to people in public places, wherever they gather," Digregorio advocates. "We are more likely to draw people to poetry if we combine exhibits of it with the visual arts, as they always draw a good crowd. Some writers' organizations are active in partnering with art organizations to showcase both poetry and art at shows."

Often, art organizations have poets write about art pieces in their exhibits.

Digregorio suggests that if poets aren't experienced in photography or other visuals arts, they can collaborate with a relative or friend who is, and have their poetry framed for an exhibit in a café, for example.

Further, the author has organized poetry festivals for national and international participants, working with municipal leaders and foreign consuls. She also organizes poetry events through public libraries and literary organizations. She was an Executive Officer of the Haiku Society of America for many years and has served as an Ambassador for The Haiku Foundation.

"It's essential to stress the benefits of writing poetry as an emotional outlet for all, including children," Digregorio recommends. "However, we must educate everyone that poetry is an art and not ramblings. It is therapeutic when it is written with thought and skill."

Digregorio encourages experienced poets to teach workshops, and aspiring poets to take them. "Experienced poets feel there is always room for improvement, and they take workshops from their peers," she says. "Experienced poets should strive to write in many poetic forms to enrich themselves, and to pass that knowledge along to beginning poets. Writing just free verse can actually be limiting, as some experienced poets do, and many beginning poets aren't exposed to other forms and the rich poetry tradition."

The author regularly gives poetry lectures/workshops at schools, libraries, and for literary organizations. These are sometimes funded by grants to organizations from Poet's House and Poets & Writers.

As for special events, she speaks at national writers' conferences and in the Midwest. She gave poetry workshops at Former Chicago Mayor Daley's After School Matters annual event. She has spoken at Career Day at The

University of Chicago and at the annual banquet of the Chicago Women's Alliance.

She has given dozens of poetry readings at libraries, bookstores, and art galleries. Her poetry has been featured on many library websites, including those of Shreve (Louisiana) Memorial Library and Mann Library of Cornell University.

"Poetry readings combined with either visual arts exhibits or with music programs, also draw a good crowd," she suggests. "And, poetry appearing on library websites during April, National Poetry Month, is especially welcomed by librarians," she adds.

The author of six award-winning previous books, Digregorio writes fourteen poetic forms, and has published more than five hundred poems internationally in journals, anthologies, and books. She also publishes short stories, and regularly writes news, features, and columns for newspapers and magazines about the literary and visual arts. She has won fifty-six poetry awards, and was nominated for a 2011 Pushcart Prize in Poetry. Her poems have been translated into Japanese, Korean, Chinese, Turkish, Polish, Russian, French, and Italian. She translates poetry books from Italian into English.

Her five reference books include three on the subject of writing to get published: *Haiku and Senryu: A Simple Guide for All; You Can Be A Columnist: Writing & Selling Your Way to Prestige;* and *Beginners' Guide to Writing & Selling Quality Features: A Simple Course in Freelancing for Newspapers/Magazines.* These books have been adopted as supplemental texts by universities throughout the U.S., Canada, Pakistan, India, and Catalonia. The latter two were Featured Selections of Writer's Digest Book Club. Her books are available through U.S. and foreign libraries, among other outlets.

Two of her other titles are: *Everything You Need to Know About Nursing Homes: The Family's Comprehensive*

Guide to Either Working With The Institution or Finding Care Alternatives and *Your Original Personal Ad: The Complete Guide to Expressing Your Unique Sentiments to Find Your Dream Person.* The former has been adopted as a supplemental text at universities throughout the U.S. The latter was a popular book in the 1990s. She also published *Shadows of Seasons: Selected Haiku and Senryu by Charlotte Digregorio.*

Digregorio is a book editor of poetry and non-fiction. She writes a poetry column, "Creatively Versed," for *Winnetka Living,* a lifestyle magazine in Winnetka, Illinois. She produced and hosted her own radio poetry program, "Poetry Beat," on Oregon Public Broadcasting. She judges national poetry and non-fiction contests.

Her longtime general writers' blog, www.charlotte digregorio.wordpress.com, is read in about 180 countries. It features the work of writers of many genres and includes author interviews, book reviews, how-to essays on writing/ publishing, and forums by writers on how creative writing matters. It also features "The Daily Haiku" by poets from about 50 countries, along with poems of other forms.

"With poetry appearing more in blogs and in columns in lifestyle magazines and newspapers, the public is gaining an appreciation for it," Digregorio says. "Published poets shouldn't be shy about contacting print and broadcast media about their work or to promote events they've organized—poetry readings, open mics, and speaking at schools and libraries," she advices. "They should also approach organizations—starting with those they have some affiliation with—to introduce poetry to their members. Art organizations are also a good start, but poets need to think beyond, by contacting healthcare/ wellness organizations and corporate workplaces."

The author was on university and college faculties in the Foreign Language and Writing Departments for several years. Prior to that, her writing career included staff positions as a reporter, columnist, and lifestyle editor at daily newspapers and as a magazine editor. She also worked as a Public Relations Director.

She is interviewed by print and radio/television organizations throughout the U.S. She has been nominated and listed in the *International Authors and Writers Who's Who*, the *Who's Who in Writers, Editors & Poets U.S./Canada*, and the *International Directory of Distinguished Leadership*.

The author thanks the journals listed on the following pages for publishing her work and for promoting healing poetry. She also thanks the general-interest publications listed for featuring her poetry. The former information will give poets and aspiring ones ideas for reading journals with healing poetry and writing for them.

She would also like to thank the libraries, cultural/ literary associations, educational institutions, other media organizations, and businesses herein that have supported her poetry. This information will provide ideas for poets to pursue comparable outlets in their area to support their poetry.

Author's Selected Publication Credits: Journals/Magazines/ Newspapers (Poems, Essays on Poetry, Columns & Commentary)

Acorn—print journal

After Hours: A Journal of Chicago Writing and Art— print

A Hundred Gourds—Australia, online journal

Asahi Haikuist Network— Japan, online journal

Asahi Shimbun—Japan, print/online newspaper

Avocet—print journal

Baltimore Sun—print/ online newspaper

Black Bough—print journal

bottle rockets—print journal

Cantos: A Literary and Arts Journal—print, Dept. of English, Missouri Baptist University

cattails—online journal

Cicada—print journal

Cornell University Humanities Division—website, poetry

East on Central: A Journal of Arts and Letters from Highland Park, Illinois—print

Failed Haiku: A Journal of English Senryu—online

Financial Times—UK, print/online newspaper

Fireflies' Light—print journal, Dept. of English, Missouri Baptist University. (Digregorio, a featured poet)

Frameless Sky—online journal & DVD

Frogpond—print journal, Haiku Society of America

Haijinx—online magazine

Haiku Canada Review— print journal

Haiku Canada Review broadsheet—print. (Digregorio, a featured poet)

Haiku Foundation, The— online journal (Archive, Per Diem, Haiku in the Workplace, Apps)

Haiku Magazine in English— Japan, online

Heron's Nest, The— online journal

Holmes County Open Air Art Museum—Ohio, online video

incense dreams—Italy, online journal

International Herald Tribune— Japan, print/online newspaper

KO—Japan, print journal

Living Haiku Anthology— online. (Includes "The Haiku Aloud" international project with Digregorio's poetry recording)

Mainichi Daily News, The— Japan, print/online newspaper

Mann Library Daily Haiku— online journal, Cornell University

Modern English Tanka—print journal

Modern Haiku—print journal

Moonbathing—print journal

Moulin Review—online journal, Brookhaven College

Muses' Gallery—Illinois, online journal, Highland Park Poetry

Never Ending Story: First English-Chinese Bi-lingual Haiku and Tanka Blog—Canada

News-Gazette, The—Champaign, Illinois print/online newspaper

New Zealand Poetry Society—online newsletter

Oregon Haiku and Tanka Society—print newsletter

Ouachita Life—Arkansas, print magazine

Point Judith Light—print journal

Prune Juice: A Journal of Senryu, Kyoka, Haibun, & Haiga—online

Red Lights—print journal

Ripples/HSA Bulletin—online newsletter, Haiku Society of America

Rockford Review, The—print journal

Rockford Writers' Guild.com—online news. (Digregorio, a featured poet)

Shamrock Haiku Journal of the Irish Haiku Society—online journal

Shreve Memorial Library—Louisiana, online poetry site

Solares Hill—Florida, print magazine

South by Southeast—print journal

Spotlights—Illinois, online newsletter, Northwest Cultural Council. (Digregorio, a featured poet)

University of Chicago—print magazine

Verse Wisconsin—online journal

Weekly Avocet, The—online journal

Winnetka Current—Illinois, print newspaper. (Digregorio, a featured poet)

Winnetka Living—Illinois, print magazine. (Digregorio, a featured poet)

Winnetka Talk—Illinois, print newspaper. (Digregorio, a featured poet)

Yoga Chicago—print magazine. (Digregorio, a featured poet)

Speaking & Teaching Engagements

Art of English-Language Haiku, The

~ Chicago Public School Teachers, Grades 3-12, (Credit Seminar)

~ Japan Information Center (Consulate General of Japan), Chicago, Illinois

~ Skokie Public Library,
Skokie, Illinois (Haikufest)

~ Winnetka Public Library,
Winnetka, Illinois
(Haikufest)

**Basics for
the Beginning Writer**

~ Willamette Writers
Annual Conference,
Portland, Oregon

**Finding Your Distinctive
Voice in Haiku**

~ North Carolina
Haiku Society,
Chapel Hill, North Carolina

**Haiku: A Path Leading
to Conservation Thought**

~ Evanston Public Library,
Evanston, Illinois (Haikufest)

~ Milwaukee Public Library,
Milwaukee, Wisconsin

Haiku at High Tea

~ Madame ZuZu's Tea House,
Highland Park, Illinois (for
East on Central Association)

Healing Art of Haiku, The

~ Chicago Women's Alliance,
University of Chicago
(Annual Banquet)

~ Northfield Public Library,
Northfield, Illinois

~ Rush University
Medical Center, Chicago
(Cancer Survivor's Day)

**How to Be a Published
and Successful Author**

~ American Association
of University Women,
Tigard, Oregon

**Introduction to Haiku
and Senryu: The Delight
of Writing & Publishing
Your Moments**

~ Arlington Green
Executive Center,
Arlington Heights, Illinois

~ Buddhist Temple
of Chicago, The
(Summer Festival)

~ Chicago Public Library
(Annual Poetry Fest)

~ Cradle of American
Haiku Festival, The,
Mineral Point, Wisconsin

~ Glenview Public Library,
Glenview, Illinois

~ Heller Nature Center,
Highland Park, Illinois

~ Highland Park Poetry,
Highland Park, Illinois

~ Japanese Consulate General,
Chicago, Illinois

~ Mayor Daley's Book Club:
Annual Spring Conference,
Chicago, Illinois

(Poetry workshops in
conjunction with the "After
School Matters" program,
Grades 7-12. At-risk kids).

~ Northwest Cultural Council,
Barrington, Illinois

~ Palatine Public Library,
Palatine, Illinois

~ Poets & Patrons
Annual Awards Ceremony,
Hinsdale Public Library,
Hinsdale, Illinois

~ The New Studio,
Evanston, Illinois

~ Vernon Area
Public Library District,
Lincolnshire, Illinois

~ Winnetka Public Library,
Winnetka, Illinois

**Polishing Your Haiku to
Be The Best for Publication**

~ Cradle of American
Haiku Festival, The,
Mineral Point, Wisconsin

**Taking The Next Step
(Writing as a Career)**

~ LitEruption Festival,
Portland, Oregon
(Authors' Panel)

~ The University of Chicago
(Career Day)

~ Tigard Public Library,
Tigard, Oregon

Tapping into Your Creativity

~ Cedar Mill Community
Library, Portland, Oregon

~ Multnomah County Library,
Portland, Oregon

~ Portland Community
College, Oregon
(Lunch and Learn Series)

Writing Artful Senryu

~ Haiku Circle
Annual Conference,
Northfield, Massachusetts

Writing for Publication

~ Barnes & Noble Bookstore,
Tigard, Oregon

~ Beaverton City Library,
Beaverton, Oregon

~ Clackamas County Library,
Milwaukie, Oregon

~ Clark College,
Vancouver, Washington

~ Delaware State College,
Dover

~ Kishwaukee College,
Malta, Illinois

~ Kiwanis Club of Raleigh
Hills, Portland, Oregon

~ Living Enrichment Institute,
Wilsonville, Oregon

~ Marylhurst College,
Marylhurst, Oregon

~ Mt. Hood Community
College, Gresham, Oregon

~ Portland Community
College, Oregon

~ Stephens College
Alumni Association of
Portland, Oregon.
("Women of Achievement,"
Annual Authors' Luncheon.
Digregorio isn't an alumna.)

~ Willamette Writers,
Portland, Oregon. (Annual
Conferences; Evening
Series Guest Speaking;
and Workshops/Lectures/
Panels).

Broadcast Interviews on Writing & Publishing

~ CCTV, Salem, Oregon

~ KEX-AM Radio,
Portland, Oregon

~ KWKH-AM Radio,
Shreveport, Louisiana

~ Moms In Business Network
(National Association
for Moms in Business),
Las Vegas, Nevada

~ Oregon Public Broadcasting,
Portland, Oregon.
(Digregorio hosted &
produced "Poetry Beat,"
a radio program, featuring
interviews and readings by
poets from multiple states.)

~ Public Access Television,
Highland Park, Illinois

~ WBOC-TV,
Salisbury, Maryland

~ WHPC-FM Radio,
Garden City, New York

~ WILM-AM Radio,
Wilmington, Delaware

~ WKEN-AM Radio,
Dover, Delaware

~ WKJN-FM Radio,
Baton Rouge, Louisiana

~ WPTE-FM Radio,
Virginia Beach, Virginia

~ WSOC-FM Radio,
Charlotte, North Carolina

~ WYUS-AM Radio,
Milford, Delaware

Poetry Readings

Arlington Green
Executive Center,
Arlington Heights, Illinois

Art Center, The,
Highland Park, Illinois

Borders Books,
Highland Park, Illinois

Brewed Awakening Cafe,
Westmont, Illinois

Chicago Public Library (Main
Library), Chicago, Illinois

Coffee Speaks,
Highland Park, Illinois

Cork and Canvas
(wine store & art gallery),
Highland Park, Illinois

Cradle of American
Haiku Festival, The,
Mineral Point, Wisconsin

Deerfield Public Library,
Deerfield, Illinois

East on Central Association,
Highland Park, Illinois

Evanston Public Library,
Evanston, Illinois

Foundry Books, The,
Mineral Point, Wisconsin

Gallery Café, Wine & Tapas
Bar, The, Westport, County
Mayo, Ireland. (Digregorio's
poetry read by the organizer)

Glencoe Public Library,
Glencoe, Illinois

Haiku Circle,
Northfield, Massachusetts

Heller Nature Center,
Highland Park, Illinois

Highland Park Poetry,
Highland Park, Illinois

Highland Park Public Library,
Highland Park, Illinois

Highland Park Senior Center,
Highland Park, Illinois

Hinsdale Public Library,
Hinsdale, Illinois

Lake Bluff Public Library,
Lake Bluff, Illinois

Libri e Letture, Milan, Italy
(Digregorio's poetry read by
the organizer)

Madame ZuZu's Tea House,
Highland Park, Illinois

Oregon Public Broadcasting,
Portland, Oregon

Patty Turner Center (senior
center), Deerfield, Illinois

Poetry Fest, Chicago, Illinois

Printers Row Lit Fest,
Chicago, Illinois

Public Access Television,
Highland Park, Illinois

Set In Stone (wine bar),
Mineral Point, Wisconsin

Trapped Truth Society
Poetry Reading, Shreveport,
Louisiana. (Digregorio's
poetry read by the organizer)

Ukranian Institute of
Modern Art, Chicago, Illinois

Vernon Area Public Library
District, Lincolnshire, Illinois

Villa Silvia Carducci, Cesena,
Italy (Digregorio's poetry read
by the organizer)

WBEZ Public Radio,
Chicago, Illinois

Westival (Westport Music
and Arts Festival), Westport,
County Mayo, Ireland
(Digregorio's poetry read
by the organizer)

Winnetka Public Library,
Winnetka, Illinois

Yummy Bowl (restaurant),
Highland Park, Illinois

Illustrated Poetry Exhibits (Solo Shows)

Arlington Green
Executive Center,
Arlington Heights, Illinois

Chicago Public Library (Main
Library), Chicago, Illinois

Fremont Public Library,
Mundelein, Illinois

Glenview Park District,
Glenview, Illinois

Meet Chicago Northwest
(Greater Woodfield
Convention and Visitors
Bureau), Schaumburg, Illinois

Moats Gallery,
Palatine, Illinois

Northfield Public Library,
Northfield, Illinois

Northwest
Community Hospital,
Arlington Heights, Illinois

Rolling Meadows Library,
Rolling Meadows, Illinois

Exhibits of Poems (Group Shows)

Arriva Dolce Gelato
and Coffee Bar,
Highland Park, Illinois

Benedictine University,
Lisle, Illinois

Bett's Apparel,
Highland Park, Illinois

Burning Bush Gallery,
Wheaton, Illinois

California State Library,
Sacramento, California

City Hall,
Highland Park, Illinois

City Park Grill, The,
Highland Park, Illinois

Columbia Association
Art Center Galleries, The,
Columbia, Maryland

Cork and Canvas
(wine store and art gallery),
Highland Park, Illinois

Corner Bakery (restaurant),
Highland Park, Illinois

Evanston Public Library
(Main Library & North Branch),
Evanston, Illinois

First Bank of Highland Park,
Highland Park, Illinois

Geneva Public Library,
Geneva, Illinois

Glencoe Public Library,
Glencoe, Illinois

Heller Nature Center,
Highland Park, Illinois

Highland Park Public Library,
Highland Park, Illinois

Hinsdale Public Library,
Hinsdale, Illinois

Holmes County Open Air Art
Museum, Millersburg, Ohio
(Permanent Outdoor Display)

Indian Prairie Public Library,
Darien, Illinois

Kennedy Memorial Gardens,
Columbia, Maryland

Lake Forest Public Library,
Lake Forest, Illinois

Library Theatre Gallery,
Bend, Oregon

Lisle Public Library,
Lisle, Illinois

"M" Restaurant,
Highland Park, Illinois

Mann Library (Cornell
University), Ithaca, New York

Northbrook Public Library,
Northbrook, Illinois

Northfield Public Library,
Northfield, Illinois

North Shore Senior Center,
Northfield, Illinois

Pace Buses, Suburban Chicago

Palatine Public Library,
Palatine, Illinois

Polish Museum of America,
The, Chicago, Illinois

Ravinia Wine Store,
Highland Park, Illinois

Shreve Memorial Library,
Shreveport, Louisiana

Sunset Foods,
Highland Park, Illinois

Warren Public Library,
Warren, Illinois

Wilmette Public Library,
Wilmette, Illinois

Winnetka Community House,
Winnetka, Illinois

Winnetka Public Library,
Winnetka, Illinois

Selected Judging of Contests

Buddhist Temple, The,
Chicago, Illinois, (Adult Haiku)

Consulate General of Japan,
Chicago, Illinois (HaikuFest
Contest, grades 3 through 12),
Chicago Public Schools.
Digregorio served as Co-Judge/
Coordinator/Organizer.

Glenview Public Library,
Glenview, Illinois
(Adult Haiku)

Haiku Society of America,
Annual Gerald Brady Memorial
Senryu Contest (Adult)

Highland Park Poetry,
Highland Park, Illinois
(Pentathlon for Adults;
Pumpkins on Parade Adult/
Student Contests; and
Poetry Challenge Haiku
Contest, Adults/Students)

Kay Snow Annual Writing
Contest, Willamette Writers,
Portland, Oregon (Adult)

Nick A. Virgilio Memorial
Haiku and Senryu Competition,
Camden, New Jersey
(Grades 7 through 12)

North Carolina Poetry Society
Griffin-Farlow Haiku Contest,
Southern Pines, North Carolina
(Adult)

Poets & Patrons Annual
Chicagoland Poetry
Competition,
Chicago, Illinois (Adult)

Skokie Public Library,
Skokie, Illinois (Adult Haiku)

Vernon Area Public Library
District, Lincolnshire, Illinois,
(Adult Haiku)

Selected Honors & Awards

Official Commendation by
Illinois Gov. Bruce Rauner
for lifelong literary arts
achievements (2018)

Pushcart Prize Nomination
by ChicagoPoetry.com Press:
"At the Museum of
Contemporary Art" (2011)

Asahi Haikuist Network (Japan)

~ Top Ten Winner,
Jan. 18, 2019:
"from the ceiling"

~ #1 Ranked Haiku,
Dec. 5, 2014:
"glazed snow on the steps"

ChicagoPoetry.com

~ Runner-Up, 2012,
Journal of Modern Poetry
Contest: "Drifting"

~ Winner, April 2010, Cram
8 Poetry Competition:
"Homeless"
(haiku sequence)

Financial Times (UK)– newspaper

~ Winner, Nov. 6, 2014, Haiku Challenge: "buried this week"

~ Winner, Oct. 9, 2014, Haiku Challenge: "commuter train"

Haiku for Hope Project (Howard County, Columbia Maryland)

~ 2013, Winner: "on the path/cherry blossoms." (Haiku exhibited at Columbia Association Art Center Galleries & Kennedy Memorial Gardens at Lake Kittamaqundi)

Haiku Society of America

~ Top 20 Winners, 2015, Nature Poetry Competition. Permanent Display of Digregorio's haiku at the Holmes County Open Air Art Museum, Millersburg, Ohio. Poem engraved on a plaque and placed on a boulder: "deep in the old growth"

Helen Schaible International Shakespearean/Petrachan Sonnet Contest

~ Third Place, 2018: "Seizing the Day"

~ Second Honorable Mention, 2017: "The Will to Write"

Highland Park Poetry, Highland Park, Illinois

~ Honorable Mention, 2018, Poetry Challenge Contest (Monster Category): "The Edge"

~ Third Place, 2017, Poetry Challenge Contest (Pioneers and Prairie Category): "Timeout on the Prairie"

~ Honorable Mention, 2016, Poetry Challenge Contest": Respite"

~ Library Exhibit Competition, April 2016: "on my bookshelf" selected for display at Highland Park Public Library.

~ Second Place, 2014, Poetry Challenge Contest (Cinquain Category): "Peaks"

~ Library Exhibit Competition, April 2014: "The Old Neighbor's Cat" selected for display at Highland Park Public Library.

~ Top 12 Annual Winner, 2014, Poetry That Moves Contest: "day's end." Displayed on placard on Pace Bus lines, Suburban Chicago.

~ Third Place, 2013, Poetry Challenge Contest: "Games With My Tomboy Sister"

~ Winner, 2013, Merchant Display Competition: "standing near the poplar" selected for store window at Ravinia Wine Shop, Highland Park.

~ Winner, 2013, Merchant
Display Competition:
"walking by sun" selected
for display at Corner Bakery
(restaurant), Highland Park.

~ Winner, 2013, Storefront
Display Competition:
"autumn evening" selected
for window at "675"
Building, Central Avenue,
Highland Park.

~ First Place, 2012,
Poetry Challenge Contest,
Non-Resident Category:
"Lost in Autumn"

~ Top 12 Annual Winner,
2012 Poetry That Moves
Contest: "Grandfather's
Death." Displayed on
placard on Pace Bus lines,
Suburban Chicago.

~ Top 12 Annual Winner,
2011, Poetry That Moves
Contest: "Seasons of the
Homeless." Displayed on
placard on Pace Bus lines,
Suburban Chicago.

~ Honorable Mention, 2010,
Funny Poems Contest:
"caught in the firing line"

~ Top 12 Annual Winner,
2010 Poetry That Moves
Contest: "Homeless," (haiku
sequence). Displayed on
placard on Pace Bus lines,
Suburban Chicago.

~ Fourth Place, 2009 Poetry
Challenge Contest,
Five Japanese-style poems
displayed at First Bank of
Highland Park and Sunset
Foods, Highland Park:

*runner in training, braving
the night, starry night,
reading yesterday's paper,
alone on the road.*

Illinois State Poetry Society

~ First Place, 2019,
Traditional Haiku Category:
"rain in late august"

~ Second Place, 2019,
Modern Haiku Category:
"alone at dusk"

~ Second Place, 2018,
Modern Haiku Category:
"easter morning/i climb to
the summit"

~ First Place, 2017,
Modern Haiku Category:
"from the open window"

~ Second Place, 2017,
Traditional Haiku Category:
"road between cornfields"

~ Third Place, 2016,
Haiku Category:
"after his death/i sit"

~ First Place, 2015,
Haiku Category:
"spring again"

~ Winner, 2015, Library
Poetry Competition: "dusk."
Haiku displayed at Highland
Park Public Library,
co-selected by ISPS &
Highland Park Poetry.

~ Second Honorable Mention,
2014, Haiku Category:
"wind blows"

~ First Place, 2013, Haiku
Category: "advancing age/
pine needles"

Mainichi Daily News, The (Japan)

~ Annual Selection Winner, 2012, Mainichi Daily Haiku Competition: "after the earthquake

~ Honorable Mention, 2011, Annual Haiku Contest: "i warm/mother's cold hands"

Make It Better magazine, (Wilmette, Illinois)

~ First Place, 2010, Poetry Contest: "The End"

Ouachita Life magazine (Arkansas)

~ Honorable Mention, 2016 Haiku Contest: "blank page"

Poets & Patrons Annual Chicagoland Poetry Contest

~ Second Honorable Mention, 2015, Chicago Art Category: "What's All the Roar"

~ Third Place, 2014, Chicago Art Category: "Urban Pasture for The Divine Bovine"

~ Second Place, 2013, Lake Michigan Waterfront Category: "The Sun Over Lake Michigan"

~ Second Honorable Mention, 2013, Chicago Art & Architecture Category: "Strangers"

~ First Honorable Mention, 2012, Chicago Art Category: "The Crowd in Chicago's Grant Park"

~ First Place, 2010, Chicago Art Category: "At the Museum of Contemporary Art"

Rockford Writers' Guild (Illinois)

~ Top Ten Winner, 2018, "Biggest" Writing Contest: "beside the eastern cottonwood"

~ Top Ten Winner, 2018, "Superstitious" Writing Contest: "intruder in my bedroom"

~ Top Ten Winner, 2018, "Winter Woes and Wows" Contest: "Winter Solitude"

~ Top Ten Winner, 2017, "Summer Headlines" Poetry Contest: "The Non-Event"

~ Top Ten Winner, 2017, "Wintry Mix" Poetry Contest: "Winter Dim"

~ Top Ten Winner, 2015, "Tan or Burn" Poetry Contest: "Just Me and the Sun"

The Haiku Foundation

~ Winner, 2014, featured on Per Diem/Website/App: "forty-fifth reunion"

Selected Publications: Articles about the Author or Those Quoting Her

Ageless NorthShore: The Daily Magazine for Chicago's North Shore—online

Art and Culture Blog, The—Illinois, Evanston Public Library

Baltimore Sun—print/online newspaper

Bottom Line/Personal—print newsletter

Byline magazine—print

California Writers Club WriteOn!—Sacramento, print newsletter

Changingcourse.com—online newsletter

Chicago Sun-Times—print newspaper, suburban edition

Chicago Tribune—print newspaper, daily and Lake County weekly editions

Complete Woman—print magazine

Daily Herald, The—Illinois, print/online newspaper

Dallas Literature Examiner—online journal

Dubai Business News—United Arab Emirates, online

Frogpond—print journal, Haiku Society of America

Haijinx—online magazine

Herald-Sun, The—North Carolina, print/online newspaper

Highland Park News—Illinois, print newspaper

IBPA Independent—print magazine, Independent Book Publishers Association

Illinois State Poetry Society—online newsletter

Independent Book Publishers Association—online newsletter

Kiwanis—print magazine

Memorie di Una Geisha—Milan, Italy, online journal

News & Observer, The—North Carolina, print/online newspaper

New Zealand Poetry Society, The—online newsletter

North Carolina Haiku Society—online newsletter

Off The Shelf—Evanston, Illinois, online newsletter, Evanston Public Library

Oregonian, The—print/online newspaper

Paperblog—France, online newsletter

Publishers' Focus—Oregon, print newsletter, Northwest Association of Book Publishers

Rebecca Review, The (Amazon)

Red Dragonfly—online journal

Richmond Times-Dispatch, The—Virginia, print/online newspaper

Ripples/HSA Bulletin—
online newsletter,
Haiku Society of America

SPAN Connection—print
newsletter, Small Publishers
Association of North America

Spotlights—Illinois,
online newsletter,
Northwest Cultural Council

Times-Picayune, The—
Louisiana, print newspaper

Tulsa World—Oklahoma,
print/online newspaper

University of Chicago:

~ Alumni Club of Chicago—
online newsletter

~ Alumni Club of North
Carolina—online newsletter

~ Arts Alumni Network—
online newsletter

~ Chicago Women's Alliance—
online newsletter

wild berries—India,
online newsletter

Willamette Writer, The—
Oregon, print/online
newsletter, Willamette Writers

Wilmette Beacon, The—
Illinois, print newspaper

Winnetka Current—
Illinois, print newspaper

Winnetka-Glencoe Patch—
Illinois-online newspaper

Winnetka Living—Illinois,
print magazine

Winnetka Talk—Illinois,
print newspaper

Wisconsin State Journal—
print/online newspaper

Writing Concepts—
print newsletter

Yoga Chicago—print magazine

Index of Titles or Opening Lines

Write Your Healing Poems Here

Write Your Healing Poems Here

Write Your Healing Poems Here

Write Your Healing Poems Here

Other Bestselling Titles

by Charlotte Digregorio

~

Beginners' Guide to Writing & Selling Quality Features:
A Simple Course in Freelancing for Newspapers/Magazines

Everything You Need to Know About Nursing Homes:
The Family's Comprehensive Guide to Either Working
With The Institution Or Finding Care Alternatives

Haiku and Senryu: A Simple Guide for All

Shadows of Seasons: Selected Haiku and Senryu
by Charlotte Digregorio

You Can Be A Columnist:
Writing & Selling Your Way to Prestige

Your Original Personal Ad:
The Complete Guide to Expressing Your Unique Sentiments
to Find Your Dream Person

~

You may contact
Artful Communicators Press with inquiries:
artfulcommunicators@icloud.com.
Phone: 847-881-2664

About
Haiku and Senryu: A Simple Guide for All

by Charlotte Digregorio

~

An altogether brilliant work. Charlotte Digregorio has penned a masterpiece!
> — John J. Dunphy, Poet and Author of
> *Old Soldiers Fading Away*

This book is overall the best one out there. The amount of information is extraordinary and exceeds that found in any other book. The author really places the keys into the hands of her readers for unlocking the mysteries and joys of haiku literature.
> — Michael McClintock, Editor, Poet, and Author of
> *Letters in Time: Sixty Short Poems*

Fantastic! I can't believe how much I learned. If a book about haiku inspires the reader to create haiku, then Charlotte Digregorio's book has done its job bountifully. If you are interested in pursuing this lovely, subtle art form, THIS is the guide you need.
> — Robin Stratton, Editor, *Boston Literary Journal*

A rich resource for teachers, concise and accessible, loaded with examples and explanations. I have used portions of the book in my introductory workshops with eighth grade students. The material is wonderfully delivered and accessible to poets and students at even this young age.
> — Tom Painting, Educator, Poet, and Author of
> *piano practice*

A must-have guide that should be on every poet's bookshelf.
> — *Authorship* magazine, National Writers Association

Your superb book covers a wide range of haiku/senryu problems. It is a foundation for the field, and I hope it deepens a mutual understanding between the United States and Japan in haiku and senryu.

— Toshio Kimura, Author, Poet and Professor
Comparative Literature, Nihon University (Japan)

Reading this book was therapeutic for me. A must-have. Passionate and clear . . . Any artist will revel in the splendor, humor, and knowledge this book has to offer.

— Connie Kuntz, Editor, *The Rockford Review*

Highly-recommended. A must-read. Exquisite examples throughout. I've read some excellent books on syllabic verse and micropoetry, but this guide truly guides.

— Mary Harwell Sayler, Poetry Editor,
Christian Poets & Writers

What a terrific book! Clear and sensible, and easy to understand. Every school should have a copy.

— Marco Fraticelli (Canada), Editor and Author of
A Thousand Years—the haiku and love letters of Chiyo-ni

Very informative and fun to read.

— Robert Witmer, Poet and Author of *Finding a Way*
Professor Emeritus, Faculty of Liberal Arts,
Sophia University (Japan)

Buy a copy. A strong overview of haiku. A wealth of material on how to introduce and/or teach haiku to children, college students and adults. Any teacher would be thrilled for the helpful guidance, examples, tools for presenting the form to the next generation. For busy teachers, the material will make it easier to provide guidance to students. The pain and work involved in creating one's own lesson plans is gone with the author's well-honed presentations.

— Michael Rehling, Book Reviewer, *cattails*

Highly-recommended book. Add this to your library, if you like the idea of learning to write haiku well.

— Alan Summers (UK), Poet and President
United Haiku and Tanka Society

Charlotte Digregorio, a best-selling writer, has produced a compendious volume offering straightforward training. With an enviable talent for detailed research and an unfounded set of organizational skills, Digregorio can lay claim to offering anybody enough know-how not only to write competent Japanese short verse in English, but see their results published.

— Lin Geary, Book Reviewer, *Haiku Canada Review*

Written by a widely-known haiku poet, experienced teacher, and leader of workshops, this is a basic guide that beginning, intermediate, and even successful, published haiku and senryu poets will find useful. . . Careful, thorough, and encouraging assistance to educators.

— Barbara Snow, Book Reviewer, *cattails*

A Writers' Blog
with Poetry for Healing

www.charlottedigregorio.wordpress.com

~

I can't compliment Charlotte Digregorio enough for her literary and artistic accomplishments, an author of international renown. Her blog is simply fantastic with marvelous poems, a gold mine for poets from every part of the world. She features poetry that leaves us awestruck, and articles that bring us together in our artistic efforts.

> — Eufemia Griffo (Italy), Poet and Author of *L'eredità di Dracula: Liriche gotiche sull'amore oltre il tempo*

Your blog is very significant, as it unites poets internationally.

> — Marco Fraticelli (Canada), Poet and Author of *Drifting*

Charlotte Digregorio is truly inspirational in the cause of haiku and poetry. "The Daily Haiku" in her blog for writers has drawn me deeper into this endlessly fascinating and rewarding genre. An invaluable resource for which I'm sure many will be giving thanks tomorrow.

> — Paul Beech (Wales), Poet and Author of *Twin Dakotas*

I am reading your lovely blog each morning. Delightful. I rejoice when I come across your haiku in journals. Thank you for your devotion to excellence in many ways, especially haiku and sharing.

> — Donna Bauerly, Poet and Author of *Raymond Roseliep: Man of Art Who Loves the Rose* Professor Emeritus, Loras College

Thank you for your admirable contributions to the creative process. A longtime follower of your blog, I enjoy your selections of poetry and educational writings.

> — Mike Stinson, Psychotherapist, Poet and Author of *extra innings*

Your blog is an amazing project! I love your site, and you are to be commended for all the wonderful work you do to promote the understanding and enjoyment of poetry.

— Debbie Strange (Canada), Poet and Author of
Three-Part Harmony: Tanka Verses

I am amazed and impressed with the bountiful treasure trove of what you share on your blog. Wonderful! I certainly am grateful for your site, and hope more people do discover the gift that it is to have a new poem featured every day and the great archive that is available.

— Tom Clausen, Poet and Author of *Laughing to Myself*

Thank you to Charlotte Digregorio for her incredible blog for writers.

— Terry Ann Carter (Canada), Author of *TOKAIDO*
Past President of Haiku Canada

Other Comments by the Author's Peers

~

Charlotte Digregorio is an exemplary supporter of the art of poetry.
— Kathy Lohrum Cotton, Poet, Editor, and Author of
Deluxe Box of Crayons

One of the most noteworthy and talented voices of the haiku panorama and poetic world.
— Maria Laura Valente (Italy), Author of *Hatsuyume: Haiku*

I highly recommend Charlotte Digregorio's enlightening poetry presentations. She really engages her audience in the subject matter.
— Judith MK Kaufman, Editor-in-Chief, *East on Central*

Experiencing the eternal energy of Charlotte Digregorio at the National Meeting of the Haiku Society of America was pretty awesome.
— Ben Moeller-Gaa, Poet and Author of *Wishbones*

Congratulations on your years of tremendous service as an officer of the Haiku Society of America. You have set the bar high for your successors.
— David G. Lanoue, Poet and Author of
Write Like Issa: A Haiku How-To
Professor, Xavier University of Louisiana
Past President, Haiku Society of America

My gratitude for your valuable service as a contest judge.
Your thoughtful selections and comments on these poems were incredibly wonderful in terms of insight and value to the authors.
It is truly an honor to have you as our judge.
— Richard Allen Taylor, Poet and Author of
Armed and Luminous
Director, Adult Contests, North Carolina Poetry Society

To Order Your Autographed Copy

Please send me_____copy(ies) of *Ripples of Air: Poems of Healing.*

($19.95 each, softcover)

Please add $4 for USPS Media Rate Shipping and Handling for one book.

(You may contact Alice Andresen about special rates for multiple/bulk orders or foreign orders.)

Name_____

Address_____

City/State/ZIP_____

Phone (_____) _____

My check, payable to Artful Communicators Press,

in the amount of $_____ is enclosed.

Artful Communicators Press
711 Oak St., Ste. 310
Winnetka, IL 60093, USA
Phone: 847-881-2664
Email: artfulcommunicators@icloud.com

Your satisfaction is guaranteed.